THE
INDISPENSABLE
GUIDE
to practically
EVERYTHING

The Bible

LARRY RICHARDS

Guideposts
New York

The Indispensable Guide to Practically Everything: The Bible

ISBN-13: 978-0-8249-4769-9

Published by Guideposts
16 East 34th Street
New York, New York 10016

www.guideposts.com

Distributed by Ideals Publications
2636 Elm Hill Pike, Suite 120
Nashville, Tennessee 37214

Guideposts and *Ideals* are registered trademarks of Guideposts.

Acknowledgments
Every attempt has been made to credit the sources of copyrighted material used in this book. If any such acknowledgment has been inadvertently omitted or miscredited, receipt of such information would be appreciated.

Scripture quotations marked CEV are from the Contemporary English Version, copyright © 1995 by the American Bible Society. Used by permission.

Scripture quotations marked HCSB are from the Holman Christian Standard Bible®, copyright © 1999, 2000, 2002, 2003 by Holman Bible Publishers. Used by permission. Holman Christian Standard Bible®, Holman CSB®, and HCSB® are federally registered trademarks of Holman Bible Publishers.

Scripture quotations marked MSG are from *The Message*. Copyright © 1993, 1994, 1995, 1996, 2000, 2001, 2002. Used by permission of NavPress Publishing Group.

Scripture quotations noted NASB are from the New American Standard Bible®, copyright © 1960, 1962, 1963, 1968, 1971, 1973, 1975, 1977, 1995 by The Lockman Foundation. Used by permission.

Scripture quotations marked NIV are from the Holy Bible, New International Version®. Copyright © 1973, 1978, 1984, International Bible Society. Used by permission of Zondervan Publishing House. All rights reserved.

Scripture quotations marked NKJV are from the New King James Version. Copyright © 1982 by Thomas Nelson, Inc. Used by permission. All rights reserved.

Scripture quotations marked NLT are from the *Holy Bible*, New Living Translation, copyright © 1996, 2004. Used by permission of Tyndale House Publishers, Inc., Wheaton, IL 60189. All rights reserved.

Library of Congress Cataloging-in-Publication Data

Richards, Larry, 1931-
    The Bible / Larry Richards.
        p. cm—(The indispensable Guide to Practically Everything)
    ISBN 978-0-8249-4769-9
1. Bible—Introductions. I. Title.
    BS475.3.R53 2008
    220.6'1–dc22

                                    2008043340

Editor: Lila Empson
Cover and interior design: Whisner Design Group
Typesetting: Educational Publishing Concepts

Printed and bound in the United States of America

10 9 8 7 6 5 4 3 2 1

As in Paradise, God walks in the
Holy Scriptures, seeking man.

Saint Ambrose

Contents

Introduction 13

A Broad View of the Bible and Its Highlights............. 17

  1. Why You Can Trust the Bible 19

  2. Faithfulness to the Original Manuscripts............... 21

  3. How Authentic Are So Many Different Versions? ... 23

  4. Ways the Bible Shapes People's Lives.................... 25

  5. Getting the Most Out of Your Bible 27

  6. Who God Is 29

  7. What Does It Mean to Be Human? 33

  8. What Makes Good and Evil? 37

  9. Life and Death and the Big Picture....................... 39

10. Wonders and Signs That Point to God 41

11. The Bible's Bottom Line Is Good News................ 43

The Old Testament and the Pentateuch....................... 47

12. Old News Is Important News............................... 49

13. What the Ancient Middle East Was Like 51

14. Everyday Life in Old Testament Times 53

15. A Time Line from Creation to Christmas 57

16. Significant Men of the Old Testament 59

17. Significant Women of the Old Testament 63

18. Events That Shaped the Old Testament 67

19. The First Five Books 71

20. Genesis—The Beginning of the Story 73

21. Exodus—The Story Continues 77

22. Leviticus—Camped at Sinai 81

23. Numbers—On the Road Again 83

24. Deuteronomy—Poised on Canaan's Border 85

The Books of History and Poetry 87

25. The Tragic Story of a Straying People 89

26. Joshua—Conquest of Canaan 91

27. Judges and Ruth—Plunge into Darkness 93

28. 1 and 2 Samuel—The Age of Transition 97

29. 1 and 2 Kings—Inevitable Decline 101

30. 1 and 2 Chronicles—
    History in Divine Perspective 105

31. Ezra and Nehemiah—Exiles Return 107

32. Esther—Insight into Providence 111

33. The Practical Poets of Scripture 113

34. Job—Story of Triumph over Harsh Troubles 115

35. Psalms—Songs of Passion, Joy, and Awe 117

36. Proverbs—Pithy Principles of Right
    and Wrong.. 121

37. Ecclesiastes—Writings of Discernment and
    Knowledge 123

38. Song of Solomon—Collection of Love Poems..... 125

The Prophets 127

39. Timely Messages from God 129

40. Isaiah—Words of Hope 131

41. Jeremiah and Lamentations—
    Light in Darkness... 135

42. Ezekiel—Darkness and Dawn............................. 139

43. Daniel—Visions of History to Come 141

44. Minor Prophets in Israel—Jonah, Amos,
    and Hosea.. 143

45. Minor Prophets in Judah—Obadiah, Joel,
    Micah, Nahum, Habakkuk, and Zephaniah 147

46. Prophets After the Exile—Haggai, Zechariah, and Malachi 151

The New Testament.. 155

47. The Centuries Between the Testaments 157

48. Life and Worship in the Holy Land 159

49. Jesus, Hero of the New Testament 161

50. Major Events in the Life of Jesus........................ 163

51. From Holy Land Faith to World Religion 165

52. Peter, Paul, and the Apostles.............................. 167

53. Grace, the Open Secret of Christianity................ 169

54. The Spread of the Gospel................................... 171

The Gospels.. 173

55. Why Four Accounts of Jesus' Life........................ 175

56. Matthew—The Gospel of the Servant King 177

57. Mark—Portrait of a Man of Action...................... 181

58. Luke—The Gospel of the Ideal Man.................... 183

59. John—The Gospel of the Son of God.................. 187

Acts, Letters, and Revelation 191

60. Acts—Growth of the Church 193

61. Romans—The Solution.. 195

62. 1 Corinthians—The Problem-Solving Epistle 197

63. 2 Corinthians—New Covenant Ministry 201

64. Galatians—Faith and Freedom 203

65. Ephesians—Understanding Jesus' Church........... 205

66. Philippians and Philemon—Praise from Prison .. 209

67. Colossians—The Real Jesus 211

68. 1 and 2 Thessalonians—Look Ahead Eagerly 213

69. 1 and 2 Timothy and Titus—
    Letters to Young Leaders 217

70. Other Early Church Leaders 221

71. Hebrews—The Superiority of Jesus 223

72. James—Faith That Works 227

73. 1 Peter—Suffering Saints.................................... 229

74. 2 Peter—Against Heresy..................................... 233

75. 1 John—Experiencing Daily Fellowship
    with God 235

76. Jude—Contending for the Faith 239

77. Revelation—The Final Triumph........................... 241

Biblical Meaning and Purpose 245

78. Intentional Creation 247

79. Significance in Human Life................................. 249

80. God's View.. 251

Among the things that are plainly laid down in
Scripture are to be found all matters that
concern faith and the manner of life.

Saint Augustine of Hippo

Introduction

Nothing is clearer in the Word of God than the fact that God wants us to understand himself and his workings in the lives of men.

David Breese

For more than three thousand years, the words found in the Old and New Testaments have enriched us. We have looked to the Bible for comfort and encouragement. We have sought and found in its passages an incomparable vision of the God we worship. We have learned the moral principles that underlie our laws and shape our consciences. We have been moved by the healing power of forgiveness and the importance of love. It is impossible to overestimate the significance of the Bible in fashioning Western civilization and our individual lives. Truly, the Bible is history's one indispensable book.

Reading the Bible can be an exciting adventure filled with discoveries that enrich our lives. In the Bible we find fresh evidences of God's love for us as individuals. We find the wisdom we need to make good choices. We find the courage to face life's most difficult challenges and the confidence needed to overcome them. As we read the Bible, we meet men and women who serve us as godly examples. Best of all, in the Bible we sense God's loving presence and learn truths about him that enable us to trust him more fully. The Bible is not only history's indispensable book, but it is also *our* indispensable book.

Yet the Bible is not easy for most readers to understand. This one volume contains sixty-six individual books written by many authors who lived at different times and in different places. Still, Christians are convinced that God inspired the words of Scripture and that in some sense the Bible is the word of God. While the Bible's authors wrote to people of their own times, their words resonate with us today as well.

> You *are* right and you *do* right, GOD; your decisions are right on target. You rightly instruct us in how to live ever faithful to you. . . . The way you tell me to live is always right; help me understand it so I can live to the fullest.
>
> Psalm 119:137–38, 144 MSG

The goal of this book is to help modern people understand Scripture as it was written and to underline the timeless truths that serve as guideposts to a blessed life both here and hereafter.

> It is impossible mentally or socially to enslave a Bible-reading people.
>
> Horace Greeley

The assurance has grown upon me that here,
in the Scriptures, at the very heart and core of our Faith,
Christians are far more at one than their outward divisions would imply.

J. B. Phillips

All Scripture is inspired by God and is useful to
teach us what is true and to make us realize
what is wrong in our lives. It corrects us when
we are wrong and teaches us to do what is right.

2 Timothy 3:16 NLT

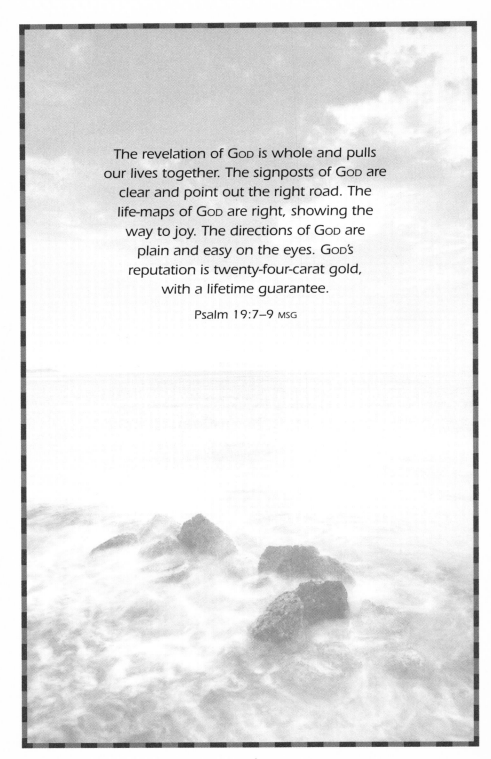

The revelation of GOD is whole and pulls
our lives together. The signposts of GOD are
clear and point out the right road. The
life-maps of GOD are right, showing the
way to joy. The directions of GOD are
plain and easy on the eyes. GOD'S
reputation is twenty-four-carat gold,
with a lifetime guarantee.

Psalm 19:7–9 MSG

A Broad View of the Bible and Its Highlights

The Bible provides straightforward answers to life's ultimate questions: Who are we? Where did we come from? Where are we going? And what difference does it make?

Contents

Why You Can Trust the Bible 19

Faithfulness to the Original Manuscripts............................. 21

How Authentic Are So Many Different Versions? 23

Ways the Bible Shapes People's Lives.................................... 25

Getting the Most Out of Your Bible 27

Who God Is 29

What Does It Mean to Be Human?.. 33

What Makes Good and Evil? 37

Life and Death and the Big Picture....................................... 39

Wonders and Signs That Point to God 41

The Bible's Bottom Line Is Good News................................. 43

I am the eternal God. So tell them that the LORD,
whose name is "I Am," has sent you. This is my name
forever, and it is the name that people must
use from now on.

Exodus 3:14–15 CEV

Why You Can Trust the Bible

The Bible is reliable and relevant. It speaks to our hearts and offers us hope. Second Timothy 3:16 explains: "All Scripture is God-breathed" (NIV). The Greek word translated "God-breathed" pictures a wind filling the sails of a ship. In a similar way, God filled the writers of Scripture so the words they wrote would convey the message he intended.

That's a stunning claim, but it fits. The Bible tells a consistent story throughout and draws an accurate portrait of flawed humanity. Best of all, in the Bible God offers a personal relationship with him, enabling us to become the persons we yearn to be.

✳

A Single, Consistent Story

It takes sixty-six books of the Bible to tell the story of God's relationship with human beings. We watch the story unfold from Genesis, the book of beginnings, on through Revelation, the book that unveils the glorious future God intends for us. The story is complex, rich in plot and subplot. It took many hundreds of years to tell and many writers to record. The only way we can explain the Bible is on its own terms. It is the "God-breathed" book, the very Word of God.

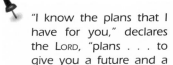

"I know the plans that I have for you," declares the LORD, "plans . . . to give you a future and a hope."

Jeremiah 29:11 NASB

Holy men of God spoke as they were moved by the Holy Spirit.

2 Peter 1:21 NKJV

The unity of Scripture—the fact that it tells a consistent story—is compelling reason to trust the Bible. But something else is even more compelling: prophecy. Again and again, the writers of the Bible predict future events. These predictions and their fulfillment knit the Bible together and create an unbreakable bond between books written in different eras by different writers.

Consider the prophecies concerning Jesus, the central figure and hero of the Bible's story. Seven hundred years before Jesus' birth, Isaiah described the virgin birth (Isaiah 7:14), and Micah placed it in Bethlehem (Micah 5:2). Isaiah also graphically portrayed Jesus' execution with criminals (Isaiah 53:9, 12) and his burial in a rich man's tomb (Isaiah 53:9). A thousand years before the event, King David wrote a psalm that recorded Jesus' dying words (Psalm 22:1) and described Jesus' being pierced by a Roman soldier's spear (Psalm 22:16). Such detailed prophecies convince us that the Bible is not simply the musings of religious men.

The Bible's story about God and humankind is epic in scope. But it's also a story about you and me. If you have wondered what life is about or experienced doubt or despair, the Bible's story is your key to peace with God and hope for the future.

Take It to Heart

The Bible's story about God and humankind is epic in scope. But it's also a story about you and me. If you have wondered what life is about or experienced doubt or despair, the Bible's story is your key to peace with God and hope for the future.

By the Numbers

2600 statements affirm that "God said" or that Scripture is "the Word of the Lord."

1545 years span the time of writing from the first book to the last.

66 "books" make up the Bible.

32 named individuals, plus others who remain unknown, wrote the Bible.

1 single, consistent message from God is contained in the Bible.

Faithfulness to the Original Manuscripts

When Moses wrote Genesis, he used a sharpened reed as a pen and ink compounded from minerals or plants. He wrote on pliant fibers or animal skin. If you could have looked over his shoulder, you would have noticed that he wrote Hebrew in a script different from modern Hebrew letters. Bible scholars call what Moses wrote the autographa, that is, "the original." Today we don't have the original of *any* book of the Bible. How can we say with confidence that a Bible passage reliably represents the original? How can we say that the Bible is "the Word of God"?

Old Testament Transmission

Most Christians assume that God supervised the transmission of the autographa across the millennia. Plenty of evidence supports this. Hebrew scribes had a system to ensure their copies of Old Testament books were perfect. As each line was written, the scribe counted to identify the middle letter. He then matched the middle letter in his copy to the middle letter in the master text. He followed the same procedure when finishing a page or an entire book. If at any checkpoint—line, page, or complete book—the middle letters did not match, the scribe would destroy the entire copy and begin again.

The commands of the LORD are clear, giving insight for living.

Psalm 19:8 NLT

My comfort in my suffering is this: Your promise preserves my life.

Psalm 119:50 NIV

Before the discovery of a copy of Isaiah among the Dead Sea Scrolls in Israel, the earliest Hebrew text of the Old Testament (OT) was the Masoretic text, which dated from about AD 1100. The Isaiah scroll was copied two to three hundred years before Jesus, and it is essentially the same as the Masoretic text. The Old Testament book had been transmitted accurately for fourteen hundred years!

New Testament Transmission

The Greek New Testament presented a different problem. Hundreds of copies were made in the first and second centuries, with less care than taken by the Old Testament copyists. By comparing early copies from different parts of the world, however, modern scholars were able to re-create an accurate Greek New Testament. One respected scholar stated that words in question take up less than a half page of a Greek testament and that no doubtful word affects a single New Testament teaching.

Myth Buster

Scholars once claimed the Old Testament text couldn't have been transmitted accurately. The discovery in a cave in Israel of a copy of Isaiah with other so-called Dead Sea Scrolls proved otherwise. Before the Dead Sea Scrolls, the earliest Hebrew text of the Old Testament, the Masoretic text, dated from about AD 1100. The Isaiah scroll was copied two to three hundred years before Christ—and it is essentially the same as the Masoretic text. The Old Testament book had been transmitted accurately for fourteen hundred years!

Check Your Understanding

- **What are the autographa?**

The autographa are original copies of Old Testament or New Testament books.

- **How do we know the Old Testament books were accurately transmitted?**

History records the care taken by Hebrew scribes making copies, and scholars have compared the Masoretic text of Isaiah with a version of Isaiah copied more than fourteen hundred years earlier.

- **How did scholars obtain accurate copies of New Testament books?**

Scholars compared hundreds of Greek manuscripts from different parts of the world.

How Authentic Are So Many Different Versions?

English is a living language that is constantly changing. The King James Bible of 1611, still read by many, uses the word *prevent* in 1 Thessalonians 4:15. While today *prevent* means "to keep from," in the 1600s it meant "to precede" or "to go on ahead of." New versions of the Bible preclude misunderstandings from changes in meaning. For instance, a popular modern version changed *brothers* to read *brothers and sisters* since the intent of the original was to include women as well as men.

However, there is an even more important reason why publishers have provided us with many different English versions.

Translation Concepts

Every English translation is an effort to make the Bible clear and understandable. In addition to updating English usage, translators are intent on finding the best way to communicate the meaning of the Greek and Hebrew originals. Some English versions, like the American Standard Version (ASV), use a *word-for-word concept*, translating each word in the originals by the same English word wherever it appear s. This is similar to the approach of *complete equivalence* taken by the New King James Version (NKJV) translators. Other English versions, like the New International Version (NIV), use a *dynamic equivalent concept*, trying to determine in context the shades of meaning of original

Whoever hears these sayings of Mine, and does them, I will liken him to a wise man who built his house on the rock.

Matthew 7:24 NKJV

These words I speak to you are not incidental additions to your life, homeowner improvements to your standard of living. They are foundational words, words to build a life on.

Matthew 7:24 MSG

words or phrases and rendering them by the English equivalent of that shade of meaning. Some English versions aren't translations at all, but are *paraphrases*, like J. B. Phillips or The Message. These versions seek to present meaning in vivid language that may not reproduce any of the original words or phrases *per se*.

The result is that today we have many English versions of the Bible, all of which are intent on communicating the message of the Bible in up-to-date language that is easily understood.

While scholars debate the translation concept that is most appropriate, all agree that modern translations provide reliable and trustworthy English versions and that paraphrases bring a vividness and immediacy to Bible reading.

Point to Remember

Today's English versions have been produced by panels of scholars who are intimately familiar with the Hebrew Old Testament and the Greek New Testament. Modern versions are reliable and relevant and can be trusted.

Check Your Understanding

- **Why is it important to produce contemporary versions of the Bible?**

It is important because the English language is constantly changing.

- **What different translation concepts are used in creating English versions?**

Translation concepts include word-for-word, complete equivalence, dynamic equivalence, and paraphrase.

Ways the Bible Shapes People's Lives

The Bible has shaped the lives of believers and unbelievers alike. Western civilization itself rests on foundations laid in this unique and influential book. Our laws are rooted in the moral vision of the Scriptures, and even in this so-called post-Christian era, our stated values continue to reflect the Bible's teachings. Moreover, educational and hospital movements, and even the American Society for the Prevention of Cruelty to Animals, were initiated by those committed to the Bible.

Lasting Influences

The f act is, our laws have their roots in the Old Testament's statements of right and wrong as defined in the Ten Commandments. Do not kill, do not steal, do not bear false witness, do not commit adultery. These and other biblical standards shape our concept of right and wrong. The laws enacted at every level of government express these standards. Simply put, the Bible is largely responsible for the social contract designed to protect citizens and punish evildoers.

> I obey your word instead of following a way that leads to trouble.
>
> Psalm 119:101 CEV
>
> Make me walk along the path of your commands, for that is where my happiness is found.
>
> Psalm 119:35 NLT

The Bible is the source of the values that undergird society: the role of the family in bringing up children, the conviction that human life is sacred, the belief that work has value and significance. These values are rooted in Scripture. It is significant that when groups complain about and denounce "traditional values," and when they complain that Christians are trying to force *their* values on society, by their very opposition the groups demonstrate that the values they rebel against are rooted in Scripture.

The Bible has shaped the concept of God shared in Western society. The God whom atheists deny and agnostics doubt isn't some abstract being. He is the God revealed in the Bible: the Creator of heaven and earth, the moral Judge and Savior of humankind. Not surprisingly, most people in Western societies also believe that death is not the end, that there is a heaven to gain and a hell to avoid.

Final Thoughts

 Men and women who were deeply devoted to the Bible fought to end slavery, established colleges, launched the hospital movement, and led the fight to end exploitation of child labor. The Bible has shaped our lives, our laws, our values, and our way of life.

Check Your Understanding

- What has made Western civilization different from other civilizations?

Western civilization is based largely on the teachings of the Bible.

- What influences has the Bible had on society?

The Bible has shaped our civilization's laws, values, and concept of God. The war to end slavery, the hospital movement, and other movements have been initiated by Bible believers.

Getting the Most Out of Your Bible

Some folks are casual readers of the Bible. They read a chapter or a passage regularly, but their reading is more of a ritual than a reflection. Other folks are serious readers. They view the Bible as the Word of God. They feel that God speaks through the Bible, and they are eager to hear what he's saying.

Reading the Bible casually is not inherently wrong. But to get the most from Scripture, we want to read seriously, seeking to understand and to respond to what God is saying to us today.

Reading Seriously

Prayer is a good first step in reading the Bible. We ask the God who shares his word with us to speak in our hearts. We ask him to use the Bible to help us understand his ways and to know him better.

Reading a chapter or a passage for understanding is a good second step. That means reading thoughtfully: Consider, what does the passage tell us about God? What does it say about human beings and about God's ideal for our lives? What warnings or promises can you find in the passage? What guidelines for living a good life are in it?

At times when we read thoughtfully we are bound to have questions. We can often find help

> We have not stopped praying for you since we first heard about you. We ask God to give you complete knowledge of his will a nd to give you spiritual wisdom and understanding. Then the way you live will always honor and please the Lord.
>
> Colossians 1:9–10 NLT
>
> The ears of all the people were attentive to the Book of the Law.
>
> Nehemiah 8:3 NKJV

to answer these questions in a study Bible (a Bible that contains notes and other helps), or in a Bible handbook or one-volume Bible commentary.

When we are satisfied that we have a reasonable understanding of the Bible passage, we can read it again for application. How does what God said apply to our lives? How do principles or direct teachings apply to us as parents, spouses, employers, employees, friends, citizens, or members of our local church?

When we sense a way that the Bible applies to our own lives, we want to respond to what God is saying to us. The goal of reading the Bible is not simply to know more, but the goal is to live better lives. As God speaks to us and as we respond to him, our lives will be enriched, and we will be drawn closer and closer to God.

Final Thoughts

God wants to develop a deeply personal relationship with us. Reading the Bible seriously, getting to know God better, and making the choices that please him are power-ful ways to nurture that very personal relationship.

Check Your Understanding

- **What steps are involved in reading the Bible seriously?**

Steps include praying, reading thoughtfully, seeking answers to questions, seeing how the passage applies to us, and responding to what God has said.

- **What is the goal of reading the Bible seriously?**

The goal is to know God better and make choices that please him.

Who God Is

To the Greek philosopher Aristotle, the concept of *god* meant an impersonal Unmoved Mover, a distant First Cause who initiated a cascading series of causes and consequences. For most ancients, gods were mysterious "mighty ones" who, except for their supernatural powers, shared the best and the worst of human nature. But we should not criticize. Many people today have no clear concept of who God is and what he is like.

No Stranger

The God of the Bible does not want to be a stranger. He wants us to know him; he wants us to know him well. We will never understand God completely. But God introduces himself to us in the Bible and reveals enough of his motives for us to learn to trust him completely.

> Jesus said . . . "He who has seen Me has seen the Father."
>
> John 14:9 NKJV
>
> This is eternal life, that they may know You, the only true God, and Jesus Christ whom You have sent.
>
> John 17:3 NASB

One way that God introduces himself to us is through his mighty acts. God revealed his power in Creation. He revealed his concern for his people in the Exodus miracles that freed Israel from slavery in Egypt. He revealed his moral character in the laws he gave through Moses. And God revealed his love for everyone through Jesus' sacrifice of himself to pay for our sins.

Another way God introduces himself is through his names. Many names associate God with a quality or characteristic that describes him. Biblical names reveal God as almighty (Genesis 17:1), faithful (Deuteronomy 7:9), righteous (Psalm 7:9), and holy (Isaiah 5:16). He is a God of justice (Isaiah 30:18) and a God of truth (Isaiah 65:16). He is humankind's Judge (Psalm 50:6), and at the same time he is our Savior (Isaiah 60:16).

God also introduces himself through images that picture his relationships with his people. God is our fortress (2 Samuel 22:2), and he is our place of safety. He is our hope (Jeremiah 14:8) who deliverers us from danger (Psalm 91:3).

No More Mystery

God also shares his thoughts and motives with us in Scripture. This is important since there is a limit to what we can know about any person by observing his actions.

Too many people who have difficult experiences or note injustices are quick to blame God and to question his motives. But when we look into Scripture, we discover that God strips many of his actions of their mystery by sharing his motives and intent.

Why did God act to free his people from slavery? The Bible says this: "God looked upon the children of Israel, and God acknowledged them" (Exodus 2:25 NKJV).

Why did God give Israel a law to live by? This is Moses' explanation: "Stay on the path that the LORD your God has commanded you to follow. Then you will live long and prosperous lives" (Deuteronomy 5:33 NLT).

Repeatedly, God explains why he chooses to act as he does. The more we read the Bible and the more we hear what God says, the more fully we are able to trust him with the things we cannot explain.

No Doubts

Even with all the ways that God makes himself known in Scripture, some people still have doubts. To allay these doubts, in a unique event God stepped into history. God became human. He revealed himself fully in the person of Jesus when he lived here on earth.

Consider the events recorded in the four New Testament Gospels, Matthew, Mark, Luke, and John. Jesus' miracles demonstrate God's absolute authority over illness, over nature, over evil spirits, and over death itself. As we walk with Jesus, however, we are impressed by far more than God's power.

We read that Jesus touched and healed a leper, and we gain a fresh appreciation for God's compassion. We read that Jesus taught about his Father, and we realize that God views us as his children. We read about Jesus' anger at the religious leaders' lack of empathy with the poor and the outcast, and we marvel at God's deep concern.

Digging Deeper

Can we trust the Gospel accounts of Jesus' life? Each of the four Gospels—Matthew, Mark, Luke, and John—is based on eyewitness accounts of Jesus' life. When Matthew and Mark penned their portraits of Jesus, thousands who had witnessed Jesus' miracles and heard his teaching were still living. Luke, who wrote some thirty years after  Jesus' resurrection, interviewed many who had known Jesus person-ally. John, who wrote some fifty years after the Resurrection, traveled with Jesus all during Jesus' years of public ministry. We can trust the picture of Jesus drawn by the four Gospel writers.

Final Thoughts

God doesn't want to be a stranger to us. He is eager for us to know who he is and what he is really like. And we *can* know God. We know this because he has revealed himself to us in his Word, and especially in his Son, Jesus. God has revealed himself in his actions, in his names, in sharing his thoughts and motives, and ultimately in Jesus. God wants us to know him and to trust him. And through the historical record that we find in the Scriptures, we can.

Check Your Understanding

• Through what mighty acts does God introduce himself to us?

God introduces himself through Creation, the miracles that freed the Hebrew slaves, the Law given through Moses, the Cross, and the Resurrection.

• Why does God often explain the motives behind his actions?

God wants us to understand, and without such explanations we might misinterpret his actions and develop false ideas about what God is like.

• What is God's ultimate revelation of himself?

God became a true human being in Jesus. The life Jesus lived among us here on earth gives us the most complete picture of God that we have available. We can read about his life in the Gospels and meet him personally.

From the very first day, we were there, taking it all in—we heard it with our own ears, saw it with our own eyes, verified it with our own hands.

1 John 1:1 MSG

What Does It Mean to Be Human?

An ancient Greek advised, "Know thyself." He wasn't giving psychological advice. He was a philosopher, encouraging people to accept their place in the world. We might paraphrase his advice like this: "Accept the fact that you're just a human being." To the Greeks, being a human meant being one of the *thanatoi*, the "dying ones," in contrast to the *athanatoi*, the undying gods and goddesses. Another interpretation is to not be too full of yourself. After all, you are nothing special. You are just another human being, destined to live a brief lifetime and then be gone. But was the ancient Greek right, or are human beings more special than he imagined?

Humans in the Creation Story

Genesis 1 relates the story of God's creation of the material universe. Then in Genesis 2 the writer goes back for a close-up look at the creation of human beings. God fashioned animals by simply speaking a word. But the Bible pictures God bending down to mold a human body from the dust of the earth. Then the Creator breathed into it the "breath of life." And, the text says, "the Man came alive—a living soul!" (Genesis 2:7 MSG).

> What is man that You remember him, the son of man that You look after him? You made him little less than God and crowned him with glory and honor. You made him lord over the works of Your hands; You put everything under his feet.
>
> Psalm 8:4–6 HCSB

This image of the creation of Adam and the subsequent fashioning of Eve from one of Adam's ribs sets human beings apart from the animals. So does the statement that God created humans in his own image and likeness (Genesis 1:26). While human beings share their physical form with animal creation, we share our identity as persons—our nature as rational and emotional beings who think and feel and make choices—with the God who fashioned us. Human beings have a foot in both worlds; the material world of the physical universe and the immaterial world of the spirit.

Because God made us in his image and likeness, humans are special. We are precious to God and distinct from the animals. Your physical body will die, but the essential "you" will exist forever, just as God exists forever.

Just a Naked Ape?

A popular book raised that question some years ago. The author answered the question "yes." He examined all the traits humans share with animals and concluded that all humans are merely naked apes.

One reason some people take this position springs from what is often referred to as man's "animal nature." These folks believe that only by assuming a "primitive" ancestry can the darker side of humans be explained. After all, enlightened humans decry humankind's ruthless traits and actions. Such things simply must be the residue of animal behaviors that humans will one day outgrow.

The Bible has another explanation. After God created humans in his image and likeness, the first humans rebelled. They rejected God by disobeying him. As a consequence of that act, humanity's original character was distorted. All those gifts God gave humankind with his image and likeness were warped and twisted. We think, but our reason is flawed. We feel, but too often we love evil and are repelled by good. We make choices, but our choices are corrupted by motives of which we're often unaware. We humans exist with one foot in time and the other foot in eternity; we live wrongly.

That is what sin is. While sins refer to specific acts, *sin* in the Bible refers to the fact that people's original nature lies in ruins. There is enough of the original construction left to recognize what we were, but the tangled wreckage of our lives makes it clear that being human no longer means what it did when God first created us.

No, Never Abandoned

Still, one thing is certain. There is enough of the image and likeness remaining to make us objects of God's love. There is enough of the image and likeness for God to redeem us. There is enough for us to renew the spiritual life that has been lost. There is enough to reshape our personalities and make us more and more what humans were meant to be in the beginning.

That ancient advice to know yourself is good advice still. But know yourself as more than another animal. Know yourself as a spiritual as well as a physical being. Know yourself as someone special, someone God cares about despite your flaws. Know yourself as someone who—apart from the renewing, transforming touch of the God who loves you—has no real hope for eternity.

Something to Ponder

Defining what it means to be human has never been easy, especially if one doesn't try to take into account our spiritual nature. After the death of Aristotle, the students in the Athens Academy, the most prestigious center of learning at the time, finally came up with a definition of *man*. Man, they said, can be defined as a featherless, hairless biped.

Take It to Heart

 To know yourself you need to take into account the Bible's vision of humans as special but tragically flawed. Then realize that God loves you anyway.

Check Your Understanding

- **What in early Genesis helps us see man as both material and spiritual?**

After God created man from the dust of the earth, he breathed the breath of life into man's body, and said man is made in his own image and likeness. Moreover, when God made man, he gave him a soul.

- **If a good God made humans, where did the dark side of man's nature come from?**

Genesis describes a rebellion against God that led to a twisting of human nature. The Bible calls this twisting "sin," which is a result of human nature and not evidence of an animal nature.

- **How does the Bible's teaching on what it means to be human produce hope?**

God continues to love humans created in his image, and he pursues us in order to restore what we have lost through sin.

God created man in His own image, in the image of God He created him; male and female He created them.

Genesis 1:27 NASB

Since the children have flesh and blood, he too shared in their humanity so that by his death he might destroy him who holds the power of death—that is, the devil.

Hebrews 2:14 NIV

What Makes Good and Evil?

Is *evil* simply the absence of good, or is it a powerful, destructive force at work in the world? Is *good* a distant ideal, or is it perhaps something that can be summed up in a set of rules? Is something good just because God says it's good? These are questions philosophers wrestle with. The Bible takes a different approach, a very personal one. We begin to understand the Bible's approach by looking at the Hebrew and Greek words chosen to express the ideas of good and of evil.

Evil, Act, and Consequence

The Old Testament concept of "evil" is expressed in the root *rá* and the many words built on it. *Rá* defines evil acts as "wicked or criminal." *Rá* also describes the impact of evil acts. The harm, pain, and distress wicked acts cause is evil too. Find words in the Old Testament that describe actions as wicked or criminal or that speak of human distress, and chances are, both are translations of the root *rá*, "evil."

I set before you today life and prosperity [*tob*, "good"], death and destruction [*rá*, "evil"].

Deuteronomy 30:15 NIV

Woe to those who call evil good and good evil, who substitute darkness for light and light for darkness.

Isaiah 5:20 HCSB

The New Testament adds shades of meaning not found in the Old Testament, and yet its view of evil is essentially the same. Evil is a *personal* concept; both the wicked acts we humans do and the pain and suffering they cause are personal.

Good, Beautiful, and Beneficial

The Old Testament word *tob* is also personal. "Good" encompasses the pleasant, the beautiful, and the beneficial. But underlying the concept in both Testaments is the conviction that while good things aren't always pleasurable, good is always beneficial.

Knowing Good and Evil

What does God have to do with good and evil? God knows both perfectly because God *is* Good. Only he knows with certainty what will benefit us and what will harm. And because God is Good, God always acts in ways that are ultimately for our benefit, even when what we experience is painful.

It isn't, of course, that the universe is all about us. It is about God. Still, those good things he does for us will ultimately bring God the greatest glory and praise.

Point to Remember

Good and *evil* speak of both actions and their consequences. God is committed to good, and the guidelines for living found in the Bible—thoughts as well as deeds—are intended to benefit us as well as others with whom we have dealings, our families, friends, and even the strangers we encounter.

Check Your Understanding

- What is peculiar about the basic biblical word for evil and the biblical concept of good?

The word for evil describes the harmfulness of the original action as well as the painful consequences of that action. The word for good is special in that, like evil, it has a personal connotation. It can describe an action as well as its pleasant or beneficial consequences.

- What do the concepts of good and evil tell us about God?

As God is Good, the actions he takes are for our benefit. God's rules for living are intended to benefit rather than harm us and others.

Life and Death and the Big Picture

Earlier we noted that human beings were created with one foot in the material world and one foot in the spiritual. As for our physical existence, we live and die in a brief span of time in the material universe. As for the essential "you" that is created in God's image and likeness, issues of life and death are spiritual and eternal. As we read the Bible, we discover the true meaning of life and the true meaning of death.

✶

No Dichotomy

Most tend to think of humans as having a body (a material part) and a soul (an immaterial or spiritual part). But Scripture portrays us as whole rather than as divided beings. In biological terms, we live for a time and then we don't; our bodies die. But Scripture often speaks of life and death from another perspective.

Often life and death refer to spiritual rather than biological realities. God warned Adam that the day he ate forbidden fruit he would surely die. He ate, and he lived on. Yet that day Adam did die spiritually. The likeness of the Creator was twisted almost beyond recognition, and Adam and his descendants were alienated from God. Ever since then, humans have entered this world spiritually dead, isolated from

> It's a wonder God didn't lose his temper and do away with the whole lot of us. Instead, immense in mercy and with an incredible love, he embraced us. He took our sin-dead lives and made us alive in Christ.
>
> Ephesians 2:3–5 MSG
>
> He who raised Christ from the dead will also give life to your mortal bodies.
>
> Romans 8:11 NKJV

God, and unresponsive to him. Without an inner transformation, we continue to exist in this state of separation from God. To die without that transformation dooms us to eternal separation, something the Bible calls the "second death" (Revelation 20:14 NIV).

Death in the Bible is an image of separation from God, and life is an image of restored relationship. In the New Testament, the impact of restored relationship with God is the gaining of eternal life. This new life guarantees an endless existence in God's presence after our bodies die.

We need to be careful when reading the Bible to distinguish when a passage is speaking about biological life and when it is dealing with isolation from God (death) and the promise of reestablishing a personal relationship with him (life).

Point to Remember

Men and women are destined to exist forever, either separated from God for all time or living in an intimate relationship with him for eternity. That is the order created by God. Separation or relationship is a decision. That decision is truly a matter of life or death.

Check Your Understanding

- **What are the two perspectives from which the Bible views life and death?**

The two biblical perspectives of life and death are the biological and the spiritual. The biological view is simply physical life and death of the body. The spiritual view deals with the soul. In this view, death is portrayed as human separation from and unresponsiveness to God, and the spiritual view of life depicts humans in a restored personal relationship with God.

- **Why is the spiritual perspective so vital?**

Because humans will exist forever, either separated from God or in an intimate personal relationship with him, the spiritual perspective is essential for understanding.

Wonders and Signs That Point to God

Most Christians are confident that miracles can happen. But many Christians are much too quick to label an event a "miracle." Not every cancer remission is a direct act of God, even when doctors cannot provide a medical explanation. The miracles we read of in the Bible have distinctive characteristics. And, perhaps surprisingly, miracles aren't something that Old Testament or New Testament believers regularly experienced. Of the thousands of years of history recapped in the Bible, miracles are reported in only three ages of fifty or so years each!

Marks of a Miracle

If you read about miracles in the Bible, several things immediately stand out. Miracles are public with many witnesses. Miracles are obviously super-natural, convincing the witnesses what they observe are acts of God. Miracles have a purpose, revealing something special about God and his purposes.

Exodus describes the first age of miracles. Through Moses, God devastated the land of Egypt where his people had been slaves for hundreds of years. The miracles forced the Egyptians to free God's people. In the process, the Egyptians as well as the Israelites were convinced that Yahweh

The Egyptians will know that I am the LORD when I stretch out My hand against Egypt, and bring out the Israelites from among them.

Exodus 7:5 HCSB

Rabbi, we know that You have come from God as a teacher, for no one could perform these signs You do unless God were with him.

John 3:2 HCSB

[God's personal name] was the one true God. And Israel was prepared to accept the Law that God then gave through Moses.

Second Kings describes the second age of miracles. Evil King Ahab and his pagan wife, Jezebel, almost succeeded in replacing Yahweh with the false god Baal as god of Israel. The prophet Elijah performed miracles that turned the people back to God, and Elisha, his successor, completed the reconciliation.

The Gospels and Acts describe the third age of miracles, performed by Jesus and, after his resurrection, by his apostles. Jesus' miracles authenticated him and his teaching, and underlined God's compassion, while the ultimate miracle—the Resurrection—declared Jesus to be the Son of God. Miracles performed by the apostles confirmed their authority and teaching as the promised Messiah of Israel was revealed as Savior of all humankind.

Final Thoughts

Wonders and signs may not happen today, but Bible miracles remind us that God is certainly able to act in our world. While he is not required to act publicly or to perform obviously supernatural acts, the God of miracles does work through natural means to answer prayer and to aid his people.

Check Your Understanding

- **What characterizes the miracles described in the Bible, and during what three "ages" were they reported?**

The miracles described in the Bible were public and obviously supernatural, and they revealed something about God or his purposes. Biblical miracles were reported during these three ages: the time of the Exodus, the days of King Ahab, and the time of Jesus and his first apostles.

- **What do the miracles of the Bible teach us?**

Miracles teach us that God is able to act in this world and that he does so on behalf of his people. Thus God can and will answer prayer, even if the answer isn't in the form of a miracle.

The Bible's Bottom Line Is Good News

The Bible is a book that believers study their whole lives and yet never fully understand. The apostle Peter pointed out that even angels, who live forever, long to master the mysteries the Bible documents (1 Peter 1:12). Yet some things in Scripture are unmistakably clear. One of these is that the Bible is a book packed with good news. Considering the nature of the world we live in and the tragedies and disappointments each of us will face, good news is welcome indeed.

Love

The Bible introduces a God who loves us. Before the Bible, humans believed that their gods might pick individual favorites, but no one imagined that his deities were actually concerned about him, much less that they deeply loved all humankind.

Then the Bible unveiled a God who stooped to shape humankind in his own likeness and image. It unveiled a God to whom each human being is important. In time, to prove that his message of love was hardly empty words, the God of Scripture stepped into earthly history. He became a human

God put his love on the line for us by offering his Son in sacrificial death while we were of no use whatever to him.

Romans 5:8 MSG

God raised Jesus Christ from the dead. Now we live with great expectation.

1 Peter 1:3 NLT

being. He lived among us. And then he died on a cross, that through his sacrifice we might be forgiven and gifted with a life as endless as his own.

The Bible's message of the love of God truly is good news.

Hope

The Bible provides us with *hope*, a word that in Scripture means a settled confidence in something that is sure and certain though not yet present. Such hope is a rare commodity in any era. We humans are subject to so much uncertainty, so many dangers that lie beyond our control. Wars ravage entire continents; economies collapse; illness and disease dash our dreams; injustice robs us of our rights; the litany goes on. Yet the Bible reassures us.

The Bible claims that the God who loves us holds our future in his hands, and that he walks with us into that future. In times of deepest despair, God remains with us to hold our hands. What's more, our God of love intends to turn every tragedy into triumph, every loss into gain. Perhaps it will not happen at this moment, but it will happen one day.

This settled confidence gives us the strength to keep on when others give up. It provides us with the certainty that beyond this world lie blessings and rewards we cannot begin to imagine. God intends for even times of terrible suffering to benefit us and others, and the future remains unclouded and bright.

The Bible's message of hope surely is good news.

Meaning

The Bible calls us to a life of meaning and purpose. In Scripture's call to love God and to serve others, the Bible opens to us a life of far greater significance than can be found in the pursuit of wealth or pleasure.

How we live here and what we do in the service of others will have an eternal significance that will echo far beyond time and into eternity. In loving God and serving others, we can find a fulfillment that those who live for themselves will never experience.

The Bible's message that our life can have meaning is more good news.

Guidance

The Bible provides moral guidance, setting before us what it calls "the path of life" (Psalm 16:11 NIV). The moral code expressed in the Bible is good news. There is a tendency today to resent biblical morality, however, and to consider that its wisdom on right and wrong restricts freedom. It's far too easy to think that right and wrong are completely relative and that any reference to the powerful moral standards as stated in the Bible are attempts to pile up rules.

> God causes all things to work together for good to those who love God.
>
> Romans 8:28 NASB

Far from being restrictive, the moral guidance provided in Scripture is freeing. God's intent has never been to rob us of something good, but rather to guide us away from harmful actions. In a moral universe, there are consequences to both good and evil moral choices. The good news is that the Bible enables us to make the choices that will benefit rather than harm us.

The moral guidance provided in Scripture is good news for believer and nonbeliever alike.

Digging Deeper

The Bible frequently gives ordinary words fresh meaning. Once *god* meant simply "an immortal." Then Scripture focused the meaning on a single, eternally existing Person who created all that exists. Once *agape* was the weakest of several Greek words for "love." Then Scripture transformed it by selecting the word to describe the selfless commitment of God to his creatures as seen in Jesus'  self-sacrifice. It is helpful to remember that concepts like *love, hope, fulfillment*, and even *morality* have been infused with new meaning by their use in the Bible. Only such transformed meanings could express how good God's good news truly is.

Dictionary

agape *(n.)* The selfless love God has for his people, as seen in Jesus' self-sacrifice.

Check Your Understanding

- **In what ways is the Bible good news, and how is its claim that God loves human beings proven?**

The "good news" in the Bible is the revealed love of God that provides us with hope, meaning, and moral guidance. We can know that God loves human beings because he came to earth in bodily form and sacrificed himself so that we could know his utter love for us.

- **How does the Bible provide hope and meaning?**

The Bible promises that God will always be with us, and that he will use everything that happens for the good of those who love him. The Bible points us to a life of personal fulfillment.

- **How does the Bible protect us from harm and provide for our good?**

The Bible provides moral guidance by defining right and wrong. We can gain all the benefits when we trust in Jesus and commit ourselves daily to living God's way.

The Old Testament and the Pentateuch

The roots of the Bible's story are sunk deep in history. God spoke to Abraham and Moses and performed miracles that freed an enslaved people God had chosen to be his own.

Contents

Old News Is Important News 49

What the Ancient Middle East Was Like 51

Everyday Life in Old Testament Times 53

A Time Line from Creation to Christmas 57

Significant Men of the Old Testament 59

Significant Women of the Old Testament 63

Events That Shaped the Old Testament 67

The First Five Books 71

Genesis—The Beginning of the Story 73

Exodus—The Story Continues 77

Leviticus—Camped at Sinai 81

Numbers—On the Road Again 83

Deuteronomy—Poised on Canaan's Border 85

The LORD your God is bringing you into a good land, a land of brooks of water, of fountains and springs, that flow out of valleys and hills; a land of wheat and barley, of vines and fig trees and pomegranates, a land of olive oil and honey.

Deuteronomy 8:7–8 NKJV

Old News Is Important News

"But it's so hard to understand. And all those names. Besides, we learned all those Old Testament stories as children in Sunday school." Too many of us seem to feel this way about the Old Testament. But the Old Testament, too, is the Bible, filled with riches for the people of God. With only a few clues of what to look for, those riches are easily available.

Clues for Reading the Old Testament

Much of the Old Testament is narrative, filled with stories. The stories aren't just for children. In them, we meet a God who is more than an abstract concept. He is a Person, who feels, who acts, and who has a personal relationship with those who trust him. And the people we meet in the Old Testament mentor us, providing examples and insights we can apply to our own lives.

Much of the Old Testament is sacred history, the story of the people chosen by God to bring his blessing to the world. This is history with a message, for the rise and fall of Israel's fortunes are linked intimately to the commitment of leaders and people to God and his ways. The history, too, mentors us, providing examples and insights we can apply to our nation and our lives.

> All Scripture is God-breathed and is useful for teaching, rebuking, correcting and training in righteousness, so that the man of God may be thoroughly equipped for every good work.
>
> 2 Timothy 3:16–17 NIV
>
> Guard this precious thing placed in your custody by the Holy Spirit who works in us.
>
> 2 Timothy 1:14 MSG

Much of the Old Testament is in the form of poetry. The poetic book of Job probes the meaning of suffering, while Ecclesiastes records the futility of a search for meaning apart from God. The practical sayings in the book of Proverbs guide daily choices, while the Psalms provide an essential guide to prayer and worship. Bible poetry also mentors us, providing patterns we can adopt to enrich our own relationship with God.

Much of the Old Testament is prophetic. It is filled with warnings and promises linked to God's plans for the future. These, too, mentor us, helping us understand the ways of God and reminding us that the way we live today has an impact on our tomorrows.

Final Thoughts

 The Old Testament is much more than a storybook filled with daring and adventure for Sunday schoolers. The Old Testament is an exciting book when it is read for relevance. Each type of biblical literature has its own values, its own way to communicate truth about God and provide guidance for our lives.

Check Your Understanding

- **What various kinds of literature are found in the Old Testament?**

All kinds of literature are found in the Old Testament, including narrative, history, poetry, and prophecy. These forms are excellent vehicles for finding the relevance in the Old Testament stories.

- **What is particularly relevant in each type of literature?**

Narrative introduces God as a Person, while the people we meet serve as mentors and examples. History teaches lessons about the consequences of choices and the importance of commitment to God's ways. Poetry provides patterns for prayer and worship as well as daily life. Prophecy reveals God's plans and purposes and warns of the dangers of disobedience.

What the Ancient Middle East Was Like

The ancient Middle East was the cultural milieu for the emergence of the Bible. The lands mentioned in the Bible have been called the Cradle of Civilization because some of the world's earliest societies developed in the fertile, crescent-shaped area stretching from Persia (modern-day Iran) along the Tigris and Euphrates rivers through Babylon (modern-day Iraq) across to the Mediterranean and along its coastline through Tyre (modern Lebanon), Aram (modern Syria), and Israel on to Egypt.

Cities, Culture, and Language

It was in the Fertile Crescent and in Egypt that agriculture was first practiced in the West. Here, too, the first cities developed. Although only about 10 percent of the population lived in cities, cities proved to be the stimulus for the development of government and culture. The rivers along which the cities grew became the routes over which traders moved. Gradually new and unusual goods and new ideas spread through the ancient Middle East.

As civilizations matured, written language developed. Although few people could read, and most written documents concerned

> I am with you and will watch over you wherever you go, and I will bring you back to this land. I will not leave you until I have done what I have promised you.
>
> Genesis 28:15 NIV
>
> Do what is right and good in the LORD's sight, so that it may go well with you and you may go in and take over the good land that the LORD promised on oath to your forefathers.
>
> Deuteronomy 6:18 NIV

contracts and business arrangements, the folktales and the accomplishments of the people were recorded. Archaeologists exploring in the region have uncovered a rich store of religious myths, poetry, astronomical treatises, laws, national constitutions, and international treaties.

Abram was a wealthy merchant in the city of Ur when God spoke to him some two thousand years before the birth of Jesus. Following God's instructions, Abram sold his businesses and outfitted his family with herds of sheep and camels and set out for the land we now know as Israel or Palestine. There Abram found a relatively uninhabited land. Through the millennia, however, this land has been a battlefield for the great civilizations that developed in Egypt.

The cultures of the ancient Middle East developed written languages in which they recorded religious myths, poetry, astronomical treatises, laws, national constitutions, and mundane records of taxes and business transactions. But the societies that developed were constantly at war, and the Fertile Crescent became a battleground on which massive armies constantly struggled for mastery.

Check Your Understanding

- **Why is the ancient Middle East called the "Cradle of Civilization," and what states that we read about in the Bible emerged from this region?**

A "cradle" pictures the beginning of life, and the societies that emerged in the ancient Middle East developed written languages in which they recorded laws, astronomical treatises, national constitutions, and so forth. Among the powerful states that emerged were Persia (modern-day Iran), Babylon (modern-day Iraq), Aram (modern-day Syria), and Egypt.

- **Why wasn't civilization an unmixed blessing for ancient peoples?**

Along with the benefits of civilization came governments, taxes, and wars between states, which were not so welcome.

Everyday Life in Old Testament Times

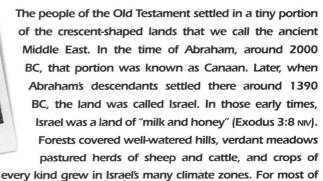

The people of the Old Testament settled in a tiny portion of the crescent-shaped lands that we call the ancient Middle East. In the time of Abraham, around 2000 BC, that portion was known as Canaan. Later, when Abraham's descendants settled there around 1390 BC, the land was called Israel. In those early times, Israel was a land of "milk and honey" (Exodus 3:8 NIV). Forests covered well-watered hills, verdant meadows pastured herds of sheep and cattle, and crops of every kind grew in Israel's many climate zones. For most of the Old Testament era, the people of Israel enjoyed a comfortable living by working the land.

Agriculture in Old Testament Times

Israel was a tiny land during most of the Old Testament era. It stretched some 150 miles north and south, with the Jordan River and the Dead Sea lying barely fifty miles east of the Mediterranean Sea. Yet the land contained fertile plains and valleys where animals could graze and where grain grew abundantly. It contained rugged mountains some thirty-two hundred feet high, with hillsides ideal for raising grapes. Olive trees flourished in the rocky soil of its easternmost slopes. A farmer's life is never easy, yet the land produced everything the people needed: dates, figs, cucum-

The land you are about to cross the river and take for your own is a land of mountains and valleys; it drinks water that rains from the sky. It's a land that GOD, your God, personally tends—he's the gardener— he alone keeps his eye on it all year long.

Deuteronomy 11:11–12 MSG

bers, onions, and various beans as well as the staple crops of grain, olives, and grapes. Even the clothing worn by the Israelites came from the land: the wool from sheep, and fine linen cloth woven from flax.

Housing

For much of the period most Israelites lived in small villages in four-room houses. One room stretched the length of the house, while the rest of the space was divided into three rooms of similar size. The houses were usually built of stone with flat, wood-beamed roofs of thatch and mud. A stairway outside the home led to the roof, where the family spent much of its time in summer. Water was supplied by a series of cisterns hewn into the rocky ground and waterproofed against leakage. The entire family slept together on a raised platform in the long room, using the outer robes they wore during the day as blankets.

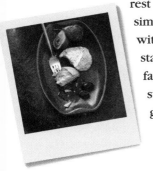

Meals

In biblical times, people usually ate two meals: a light breakfast of bread or fruit in midmorning, and a large meal about sunset. Meat was a rarity; protein was provided by dried fish, cheese, yogurt, and a variety of nuts. Figs and raisins were abundant, and barley, as well as wheat, was usually available. These were supplemented by a variety of fruits and vegetables.

The Religious Year

While life in Old Testament times was patterned by the agricultural cycle, the life of God's Old Testament people was also patterned by their religion. The seventh day of each week was set aside for rest. In addition, annual religious feasts and festivals called God's people to turn from their labors to focus attention on the Lord. March (*Nisan*) featured the Passover and the weeklong Festival of Unleavened Bread. The Feast of Weeks, a harvest festival, was held the sixth of April (*Iyyar*). The first of September (*Tishri*) was Rosh Hashanah, New Year's Day, followed on the tenth by the Day of Atonement and the fifteenth through the twenty-second by the Feast of Tabernacles. Additional festivals marking historic events were added to these specifically commanded religious holidays.

Life Patterned by Law

While the seventh-day rest (the Sabbath) and the religious festivals kept the focus of the people on God, the Old Testament contained many laws serving the same purpose. The Law specified what could and could not be eaten. The Law defined appropriate clothing, down to the tassels that were to be worn on outer garments. The Law established how God's people were to deal with various crimes, and how the people might restore a harmonious relationship with God should they sin. From birth to death, the Old Testament people were guarded by the Law. The Law provided a pattern for a holy, healthy, and harmonious life.

> Your fields were rich with grain. Olive trees grew in your stony soil, and honey was found among the rocks.
>
> Deuteronomy 32:13 CEV

> Truth springs up from the earth, and righteousness smiles down from heaven. Yes, the LORD pours down his blessings. Our land will yield its bountiful harvest.
>
> Psalm 85:11–12 NLT

Broken Patterns

At first it seems strange when we read the Old Testament to discover that many of its pages are filled with tragedy. But then we remember that the idyllic pattern of life described above depended on faithful commitment to God and his ways. Often generations of Israelites turned from God to worship idols. Then God withheld the rain or permitted foreign enemies to invade Israel. Life in Israel was disrupted by disaster—until the people realized that their sin was the cause of their suffering and they returned to God. Then God forgave them and restored the blessings so intimately linked with life in the land.

Point to Ponder

God provided his people with a fruitful land where all their needs would be met. Yet repeated failure to trust God disrupted the comfortable and blessed life God intended them to lead. It was only when they realized their failure that they were once more able to enjoy the land as God intended.

Gezer Calendar

An early inscription on a stone tablet known as the Gezer calendar outlines the yearly agricultural cycle:

Two months—[olive] harvest
Two months—planting [grain]
One month—hoeing up of flax
One month—harvest of barley
One month—harvest and feasting
Two months—vine tending
One month—summer fruit

Daily life in Israel followed the needs of the land. The pace and cycle of each year remained stable, and life on the land fell into a comfortable routine.

Check Your Understanding

▪ What was special about the land of Israel?

Though small, its varied climate zones made possible the growing of a full range of crops.

▪ Where did most Israelites live during Old Testament times, and what did they eat?

Most Israelites lived in small villages, in small four-roomed houses, where most worked the land for a living. Their diet consisted of the staples of grain, olives, and grapes. Foods derived from these staples were supplemented with a variety of vegetables and fruit. Meat was seldom eaten.

▪ What two things patterned the lives of God's Old Testament people, and were their lives ever disrupted?

The two things that patterned the lives of Old Testament people were the agricultural year and God's law. Special days were set aside for worship and celebration, and these regulated daily life. When a generation turned from God, however, God brought droughts or permitted foreign enemies to invade, until his people turned back to him.

A Time Line from Creation to Christmas

The Bible assumes that the people who populate its pages really lived, and that events described actually happened. The following chart links biblical people and events to contemporary people and events around the world.

✴

The dates for biblical people and events are derived from internal evidence—that is, dating information derived from the Bible itself. Neither biblical nor extrabiblical dates can be established with absolute precision. Yet there is significant cross-referencing—for instance, the ten kings of Israel and Judah are also mentioned in Assyrian records—to be confident of the relative accuracy of the dates chosen.

Chronology of the Old Testament

Biblical Event	BC Date*	World Event
Abraham is born	2166	Pottery introduced in pre-Inca South America
		Oldest picture of skiing carved in Norway
Abraham enters Canaan	2091	Bronze age begins in Europe
Isaac is born	2066	Cinnamon reaches Arabia from China
Jacob is born	2006	Maize (corn) is staple food in South America
Joseph is taken	1898	Pictograph writing develops in China
Joseph is made vizier of Egypt; later Israelites are enslaved in Egypt	1883	Stonehenge is constructed
Moses is born	1527	Hindu Vedas (sacred texts) are begun
Moses frees Israelites	1446	Primitive Greek alphabet is developed

Biblical Event	BC Date*	World Event
Law is given at Mount Sinai; Moses pens first five Old Testament books	1445	Sale of beer is regulated in Egypt
Israelites are under Joshua	1390	Hittites use guitars, lyres, and trumpets in worship
Judges rule in Israel	1316	Silk fabrics are made in China
Saul becomes king	1043	Lapita peoples canoe over thousands of miles to colonize South Pacific Islands
King David establishes Jerusalem as capital city;	1003	Greeks adopt the Phoenician alphabet
Solomon becomes king;	970	Chinese math textbook includes geometry
Israel becomes a major power; Jerusalem temple is finished	959	Caste system develops in India
Solomon dies and kingdom is divided	930	Carthage is founded; Pinto Indians in California live in wood huts
Assyrians crush Israel	722	Rome is founded in 753
Babylonians crush Judah, raze Jerusalem temple, and deport Jews to Babylon	586	Aesop tells his fables; Solon's law code is instituted in Athens; in Greece Thales predicts an eclipse
Jews return from Babylonian captivity	538	Book publishing begins in Greece; Buddha, Confucius born twenty years earlier
Jews dedicate new temple	509	Romans found the republic; democracy established in Athens
Last book of Old Testament (Malachi) is written	429	Plato is born

*Scholars disagree on many dates. The dates selected best fit biblical chronology.

Significant Men of the Old Testament

The Old Testament is filled with stories of all sorts of people—heroes and villains, wise men and foolish, good and evil. Each of them is available to us in the Bible, and most of their stories teach life lessons we can apply today. We learn from them; we're made wiser by the consequences of the choices they make for good or for ill. In their capacity to mentor us, most of the men of the Old Testament are significant. But there are a few individuals who stand out; men who were pivotal in setting the direction of sacred history.

Adam

Few pages of Scripture are devoted to Adam. Yet the conscious choice he made to disobey God set human history on a tragic course. Adam's choice warped and twisted not only his own nature but also the nature of his descendants. We inherit our bent toward sin from Adam, and his choice is the root from which all human misery has sprung.

Yet Adam is more than the flawed individual whose likeness is stamped so indelibly on humanity. Adam serves as a backdrop against which to place Jesus. As with Adam we know sin, the apostle Paul reminded us in his letter to the Romans, so with Jesus are all made alive through freedom from sin. From the beginning, the curse introduced by Adam was destined to be lifted and humankind's lost innocence restored.

I will remember my covenant with Jacob and my covenant with Isaac and my covenant with Abraham, and I will remember the land.

Leviticus 26:42 NLT

I have found David the son of Jesse, a man after My heart, who will carry out all My will.

Acts 13:22 HCSB

You can read about Adam in the first four chapters of Genesis, and about Jesus as Second Adam in Romans chapter 5.

Abraham

Abraham has a major role in the book of Genesis, and the rest of the Old Testament is devoted to tracing the history of his descendants. Abraham's story began when God spoke to him as an old man, making him unusual promises and telling him to leave his homeland. Abraham listened, and finally arrived in Canaan, the land we know today as Palestine or Israel. There, when he was nearing one hundred, Abraham questioned God. How

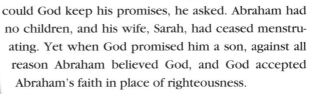

could God keep his promises, he asked. Abraham had no children, and his wife, Sarah, had ceased menstruating. Yet when God promised him a son, against all reason Abraham believed God, and God accepted Abraham's faith in place of righteousness.

The promises that God made Abraham are known as the Abrahamic covenant. They lay out the purposes God intends to accomplish in human history. Even more, Abraham's act of faith revealed that sinful human beings can be reconciled to God simply and only by trusting God's promises.

You can read about Abraham in Genesis 12–25, and the significance of his faith response to God is recorded in Romans chapter 4.

Moses

Some six hundred years later, Abraham's descendants were living as slaves in Egypt. God chose a man named Moses to win their freedom. Moses then led the freed slaves to a wilderness beneath Mount Sinai, where God gave him the Law, which has governed the lives of his people from that day to our own. At Sinai God used Moses to establish a worship system featuring a priesthood and sacrifices intended to restore individuals who violated God's law. From that day to this, Moses has been honored not only as the deliverer of the Jewish people from slavery but also as their lawgiver.

Moses' story spans four books of the Old Testament—Exodus, Leviticus, Numbers, and Deuteronomy. In those books Moses is displayed as a humble and very real human being who struggled with the burden of leading a reluctant and often hostile people. His life was a rich source of insights for maintaining a close walk with God despite stress and disappointment.

You can read about Moses and his accomplishments in Exodus through Deuteronomy. And you can discover the true significance of the worship system he established by studying the New Testament book of Hebrews.

David

Four hundred years after Moses, David rose from shepherd boy to king of Israel. He molded a disunited people into a powerful nation, expanding the land controlled by Israel some ten times. Although David was flawed, he had a heart for God and wrote many of the psalms found in the Old Testament. Most significantly, God promised David that a descendant of his would rule a worldwide kingdom forever, a promise that was to be fulfilled in Jesus.

> There are different gifts, but the same Spirit. There are different ministries, but the same Lord. And there are different activities, but the same God is active in everyone and everything. A manifestation of the Spirit is given to each person to produce what is beneficial.
>
> 1 Corinthians 12:4–7 HCSB

David's story, too, is a rich source of insight for living a godly life. His story is found in 2 Samuel; 1 Kings; and 1 Chronicles in the Old Testament. And the entire New Testament is about David's descendant Jesus.

Digging Deeper

The Great Man theory suggests that certain individuals play pivotal roles in the history. Others theorize that the development of technology or some other factor is critical and that if the Great Man were absent another individual would inevitably take on his role. Sacred history seems to support the Great Man theory. It reminds us that God

calls each believer to a unique role in life, giving him or her the gifts needed to make the intended contribution. Adam, Abraham, Moses, and David certainly were significant. So are you. The life you lead and the choices you make truly count.

Check Your Understanding

- **What is the value in looking closely at the lives of Bible people, and what makes some Bible men more significant than others?**

Most of the people in the Bible provide examples and insights that we can apply to our lives, such as devotion, obedience, and mission. Noteworthy and influential Old Testament men were used by God to transmit God's plan for living. These men—men like Adam, Abraham, Moses, and David—stand out for having played pivotal roles in sacred history.

- **What's significant about Abraham?**

God chose Abraham to receive a covenant now known as the Abrahamic covenant. The remainder of the Old Testament is the story of Abraham's descendants and his faith. His life and faith present a model for ours.

- **What's significant about Moses?**

God used Moses to free the Israelites from slavery in Egypt. Through Moses, God gave the Israelites his law and established Israel's worship and sacrificial systems.

Significant Women of the Old Testament

The women of the Old Testament lived in a patriarchal society that limited their opportunities in many ways. Yet women whose stories are found within the pages of the Old Testament remind us that women are significant in every culture and that other women may shatter the stereotype and win recognition for their exceptional gifts. While prominent women such as Eve and Moses' sister Miriam and Abraham's wife Sarah are better known, we gain an even richer understanding of women in Old Testament times by looking at several who are lesser known.

The Noble Wife of Proverbs 31

Some twenty-two verses in Proverbs 31 describe the wife of "noble character." She is portrayed going about household tasks, including managing a staff of servants, buying and selling products of her labor, and even purchasing a field. What's striking is that in the agrarian society of ancient Israel, the tasks for which she was praised within the household were the

I'll pour out my Spirit on those who serve me, men and women both.

Acts 2:18 MSG

same kinds of tasks her husband would have undertaken in the fields. Both were businesspeople, actively contributing to the welfare of the family. And the wife's skills and dedication were praised by the community as well as by her husband.

There is no hint here of inferiority, even though husband and wife operated in different realms. The household provided a context in which a woman could use all her talents and abilities, and find personal fulfillment as well.

The wife of noble character is a reminder that it was possible for women to find fulfillment despite the limitations imposed by culture.

You can read about the noble wife in Proverbs 31:10–31.

Abigail

Abigail's husband insulted David, and David vowed revenge. When Abigail heard, she hurriedly saddled donkeys and rushed to head David off. She met him at the head of four hundred warriors intent on killing her husband and his herdsmen. Abigail greeted David respectfully, but then she bravely confronted him. She pointed out that David's intention of taking revenge was both wicked and foolish. Surprisingly, David listened. Abigail was right. Despite the fact that David had sworn to take revenge in front of his men, David changed his mind.

Later, when Abigail's husband had a stroke, David married her. A strong man, he valued rather than was threatened by a woman who was equally strong. Many an Old Testament wife had as significant an influence over her husband as Abigail had over David.

Even in Old Testament society a woman's influence was a function of her character and her relationships.

You can read about Abigail in 1 Samuel 25.

Deborah

For several hundred years after the conquest of Canaan, the Israelites were governed by judges, governors who served as political, military, judicial, and spiritual leaders. One of those individuals who led Israel was Deborah.

In Israel's patriarchal society, the head of government was invariably male. Yet Deborah was so deeply respected that she was the acknowledged leader of several of Israel's tribes. The general leading Israel's forces, Barak, even refused to go into battle unless Deborah accompanied the army.

For all who today argue that spiritual leadership is exclusively for males, Deborah is a reminder that traditions and stereotypes too often serve to limit God, who created both sexes in his image and likeness and who gave dominion to both sexes (Genesis 1:26–27). Deborah stands with other prophets of the Old Testament as a reminder that culture cannot be allowed to limit the role of women whom God calls to leadership.

> God created man in his own image, in the image of God he created him; male and female he created them.
>
> Genesis 1:27 NIV
>
> Charm is deceitful and beauty is passing, but a woman who fears the LORD, she shall be praised. Give her of the fruit of her hands, and let her own works praise her in the gates.
>
> Proverbs 31:30–31 NKJV

You can read about Deborah in Judges 4 and 5.

Esther

Esther was a young Jewish girl who lived with her uncle in the capital of the Persian Empire. When the Persian ruler deposed his queen, Esther won a competition to succeed her. About the same time, an influential member of the Persian court decided to wipe out the Jewish race and won the emperor's permission. Bravely risking her own life, Esther thwarted the plot and saved her people.

The event is still celebrated by the Jewish people, and Esther is honored as a woman who used the opportunity her position provided. Every role a woman has in life provides some opportunity to serve God and others.

You can read about Esther in the Old Testament book of Esther.

Digging Deeper

Be sensitive to the clues in Scripture that show equal respect for men and women. Abraham is honored for risking all and leaving his homeland to move to "the land where you live as an alien" (Genesis 28:4 HCSB). Teenage Rebekah (Genesis 24) displayed the same faith when she left her home and family to go to Canaan and marry Abraham's son Isaac. When Josiah discovered a lost Book of the Law, he went not to the prophet

Habakkuk, a contemporary, but to the prophetess Huldah (2 Chronicles 34:19–22).

Final Thoughts

 It's too easy to conclude that women in the Old Testament were repressed by men. But that simply is not so. To characterize women as irrelevant or oppressed in the Old Testament's patriarchal society is to read contemporary prejudices into Scripture rather than to see the reality. Then as now, women were truly significant.

Check Your Understanding

- **Under what limitations did Old Testament women live, and did women have an opportunity for personal fulfillment?**

Many roles in the Old Testament could be pursued by either men or women. In addition to their role in child bearing and rearing, women in an agrarian society were major contributors to the family welfare. Women were recognized for having the same kinds of talents and abilities as men.

- **Were women strictly forbidden to fill all male leadership roles?**

No. A few roles, however, were reserved for men. Even though she couldn't be a priest, for instance, Deborah was a political as well as a spiritual leader, and some women were recognized as prophets.

- **How did women exert an influence in Old Testament times?**

Women exerted an influence in Old Testament times primarily by force of character and wisdom and by operating within their culturally defined roles. Many stories indicate that God honored in women the same qualities he honored in men.

Events That Shaped the Old Testament

The Old Testament traces the gradual unveiling of a path that leads to the fulfillment of a divine plan. In theology, this gradual unveiling is given the name *progressive revelation*, suggesting that as history unfolds more and more is known of God and his purposes. The events that shape the Old Testament are sacred history's major turning points; moments in time during which the veil that once masked God's intent is drawn back further, permitting fresh glimpses into the meaning of what has been and what lies ahead. Such major events are chronicled here.

Creation

The Old Testament constantly looks back to Creation. The Creation story in Genesis 1 defines God as a Person separate from the material universe, the source of all that exists. Old Testament faith stood in awe of such a God and found the power and wisdom displayed in Creation a constant source of comfort.

Everything I prophesied has come true, and now I will prophesy again. I will tell you the future before it happens.

Isaiah 42:9 NLT

I am GOD, the only God you've had or ever will have—incomparable, irreplaceable—from the very beginning telling you what the ending will be, all along letting you in on what is going to happen, assuring you, "I'm in this for the long haul, I'll do exactly what I set out to do."

Isaiah 46:9–10 MSG

The Genesis Flood

The flaw in human nature drives human beings to a totally corrupt civilization. Genesis 6 depicts God's decision to wipe out a generation marked by imaginations that were "only evil continually" (verse 5 NKJV). The Flood story reveals God as a moral Judge who will not let wickedness and evil go unpunished.

The Covenant with Abraham

Generations later, God selected an aged man named Abram. God gave him promises that stated clearly what he intended to accomplish in history. The means God would use were unclear, but his commitment to Abram's descendants and his intent to make those descendants a blessing to all humankind were unmistakable. The covenant promises are stated in Genesis 12:1-3, 7 and are restated in various forms throughout the Old Testament.

The Exodus: Redemption from Slavery

Abraham's descendants were enslaved in Egypt. God acted to break the bonds that held them and led them to freedom in their own land. The Exodus miracles provided this people, the Israelites, with proof that God was able to act in the world of space and time. His mighty acts armed them with the conviction that God intended to exercise his power on behalf of his people. The story is found in Exodus 5-12 and celebrates God as the Redeemer of his people.

The Giving of the Law

Once free, the Israelites were given a law that defined how to maintain harmonious relationships with God and with one another. The Law also included a priesthood and a system of sacrifices intended to restore relationships broken by violating the Law. Both the sweeping principles embodied in the Ten Commandments and the detailed applications illustrated in biblical case law provided guidance for daily living. The book of Exodus, beginning with chapter 19, contains the first statement of this law.

The Conquest of Canaan

The fulfillment of the Abrahamic covenant depended on Abram's descendants possessing the land, which was then known as Canaan (modern Israel and Palestine). The Israelites conquered this Promised Land under Joshua and took possession. Although control of the land was intermittent, the Old Testament assumes that God's purposes would be achieved only when Israel possessed its land. The story of the conquest is found in the book of Joshua.

Israel Becomes a Nation

For centuries, the Israelites lived in Canaan as disjointed tribal groups. Then under King David the people were unified as a single nation. Jerusalem became the political and religious capital of the united nation, with greatly expanded territory and power. This golden age of monarchy and national ascendancy prefigured a time when Israel was destined to be the earth's preeminent nation.

> I know the thoughts that I think toward you, says the LORD, thoughts of peace and not of evil, to give you a future and a hope.
>
> Jeremiah 29:11 NKJV

The Davidic Covenant

God expanded on the Abrahamic covenant by promising King David that his descendant would rule an ascendant Israel at history's end. This king, known as the Messiah (the "anointed ruler"), would establish an eternal kingdom.

The Fall of the Divided Kingdom

After the deaths of David and his son Solomon, the kingdom of Israel split into two independent nations, north and south, Israel and Judah. Over the centuries, the people of each kingdom strayed from God. In the end, each kingdom fell to powerful northern empires, and the Israelites were deported from their homeland.

The New Covenant

At the darkest point in the history of the southern kingdom of Judah, the prophet Jeremiah was given a promise that expanded further on the

Abrahamic covenant. In the future, the Israelites would again possess their land and be ruled by the Messiah. In that future, God would transform the hearts of his people, restoring the innocence that was lost when Adam and Eve sinned. Then and only then will the whole world know peace, and God will reign on earth.

Digging Deeper

 The Old Testament was written over a period of about one thousand years, from approximately 1450 BC to 400 BC. Over that span of time, events took place that gradually unveiled how God intended to fulfill his purposes in history. Creation affirms that the universe had a beginning. The significant events chronicled in the Old Testament assure us that the universe has meaning and purpose and that events unfold according to a plan that will lead to God's intended end.

- **What Old Testament events are significant and give shape in sequence to Bible history?**

Significant events in the Old Testament progressively unveil more about God and his purposes. These events provide the historical framework on which Scripture is constructed. Shaping Bible history, in sequence, are the Creation, the Flood, the Abrahamic covenant, the redemption from slavery, the giving of the Law, the conquest of Canaan, the establishment of the monarchy, the Davidic covenant, the fall of the divided kingdom, and the new covenant.

- **What is the value of knowing the significance of these events?**

Knowing the significance of these events provides us with a framework that gives structure to the Old Testament and orients us as we read it.

- **What do these events contribute to the personal faith of believers?**

They remind us of who God is, they give us confidence that God is in control, and they assure us that our future is secure.

The First Five Books

The first five books of the Bible are called the *Pentateuch,* which means "the five books." They are also called the Books of Moses, the Law, and the Law of Moses. Whatever one calls them, these earliest books of the Bible ascribed to Moses lay the foundation on which both the Old and the New Testaments rest. Apart from the stories told in Genesis, Exodus, Leviticus, Numbers, and Deuteronomy, the gaps in our knowledge of God would be too vast to cross.

Date and Authorship

Tradition tells us that Moses wrote the bulk of the Pentateuch, a stance assumed in the books themselves. Working from the Bible's internal chronology, Moses would have written the books within a span of some fifty years, from approximately 1450 BC to 1400 BC. Moses wrote from personal experience; these books relate his own experiences with God and with the Israelites whom he led for four decades.

We know for sure that God spoke to Moses.

John 9:29 MSG

He taught his Law to Moses and showed all Israel what he could do.

Psalm 103:7 CEV

Genesis

The first of the five books, Genesis, looks far back in time, recording events either revealed directly by God or imbedded in the folktales of the Israelites' ancestors. Whatever their source, archaeological discoveries testify to the accurate depiction of the settings within which the stories are told.

The first eleven chapters of Genesis deal with prehistory, including a unique Creation story and a vivid account of a worldwide Flood. Chapter 12 of Genesis introduces a man named Abraham, and the rest of the Old Testament is about this man and his descendants.

Exodus, Leviticus, Numbers, and Deuteronomy

The next four books relate events that took place within the fifty-year span during which Moses delivered and then led the Israelites. They describe the transition of the Israelites from an unruly mob to a disciplined people, from a rebellious and unappreciative rabble to a people dedicated to wholly following God.

In the process of this transformation, God through Moses gave the Israelites a law to live by, and he established a worship system and way of life that set this people apart from every other people on earth.

Final Thoughts

In these five books God revealed himself to be unlike the gods worshiped by other ancient peoples, gods who were part of the creation rather than its Creator. The nature and character of the God of the Pentateuch, and his relationship with human beings, contradicted rather than evolved from contemporary cultures.

Check Your Understanding

- **What are various names given the Bible's first five books, and who wrote them?**

The first five books of the Bible are variously called the Pentateuch, the Books of Moses, the Law, and the Law of Moses among other names. Moses is the author of these five books.

- **What is the source of the stories in the book of Genesis?**

The source for the stories in Genesis is either direct divine revelation or Israelite folktales.

- **What is the source of the stories in the other four books?**

The source for the stories in the four remaining books of the Pentateuch is the direct experiences of Moses himself.

Genesis—The Beginning of the Story

Every story has a beginning. Good beginnings include several important features. Good beginnings introduce and describe the cast of characters. They introduce a tension that the story must resolve. Good beginnings hint at problems that must be solved if the tension is to be resolved. Later, as the story is told, complications and subplots can be introduced. But the basic elements of the story are established in the very beginning. Genesis does exactly this for the epic story told in the Bible. To understand the story—to understand the Bible itself—we need to look carefully at the beginning.

The Cast of Characters

The Creator. Chapter 1 of Genesis introduces God as Creator. We see him create simply by speaking, and we are impressed by his power and the fact that he exists independently of the material universe.

> God created men and women to be like himself. He gave them his blessing and called them human beings.
>
> Genesis 5:1–2 CEV
>
> Noah did everything as the LORD commanded him.
>
> Genesis 7:5 NLT

Humans. In chapter 2 we're surprised to see God create the first human being, Adam. The Creator stooped to fashion a body from dust and then breathe life into his form. The man is clearly special to the Creator; he is said to be formed in the Creator's image and likeness (Genesis 1:26). In time, the Creator fashioned a bride for Adam, and he often visited the couple in a beautiful garden he designed for them.

Satan. In chapter 3 the harmony and peace of couple and Creator were shattered by a being who tricked Adam and Eve into violating the Creator's one command. Much later we learn that Satan is an evil spirit being who, ages before Adam's creation, rebelled against the Creator.

The Tension

When Adam and Eve violated the Creator's command, their natures were warped and twisted. The first pair's harmony with the Creator became discord, and confidence in his love became fear. In the grip of guilt and shame, Adam and Eve tried to hide. But the Creator searched them out. He explained the consequences of their act of disobedience, consequences that become increasingly clear in chapters 4 through 9 of Genesis.

Our first hint of the terrible impact of Adam and Eve's disobedience is seen when one of their sons murders his brother. Later another descendant violates the Creator's plan by taking two wives and justifying yet another murder. As time passes, the offspring of the first pair forget their first parents' relationship with the Creator. They follow the passions of their twisted natures until their "every intent" is "only evil continually" (Genesis 6:5 NKJV).

At this point, the Creator is revealed as a moral Judge. He decrees a massive flood that wipes out the corrupt civilization, but he preserves one family to continue the human race.

The tension that needed to be resolved was clearly defined. Warped and twisted because of Adam and Eve's initial disobedience, human beings seemed doomed to ignore God and to selfishly harm one another. Left to themselves, morally warped humans ignored God and injured one another. God was forced by his commitment to righteousness to punish them. Would God find a way to reestablish his initial relationship with humans? And would there be a way for humans to reverse the impact of the first disobedience and be made whole?

What Lies Ahead

Genesis doesn't reveal the solutions to the problems it poses. But it does offer hope. As the first installment of the story continues, God calls a man named Abram and makes several promises to him. Through this man, whose name was later changed to Abraham, God would bless all humanity. The promise, made legally binding by the establishment of what is called a covenant, passed from Abraham to his offspring, who were to become the Jewish people. Genesis 12–50 traces the passing of the covenant promises to Abraham's son, grandson, and great-grand-children. Subsequently, as the centuries unfolded and the Bible contin-ued the story of Abraham's offspring, God's solution was worked out in history.

The Promise to Abraham

God gave this promise to Abraham: "I will make you into a great nation and I will bless you; I will make your name great, and you will be a bless-ing. I will bless those who bless you, and whoever curses you I will curse; and all peoples on earth will be blessed through you" (Genesis 12:2–3 NIV).

God told Abraham: "leave you country, your family, and your father's home for a land that I will show you." . . . So Abraham left just as GOD said.

Genesis 12:1, 4 MSG

Oh, there will be suffering, for humans are willful and prone to reject God's ways. But even in the darkest of times, the promise of future blessing provides a reason to hope.

The Date

Events in the first eleven chapters are undated. Events in chapters 12–50 took place from around 2100 BC to 1800 BC and are filled with details about cultural practices authenticated by archaeology. Moses wrote Genesis around 1450 BC.

Something to Ponder

As we read Genesis, we realize that the Bible's story is *our* story. We understand that the pain we experience and cause others has its origin in what happened long ago in the beginning. Yet the Bible offers us hope, for God has solved the problems that Genesis poses, and in the Bible we will discover our glorious destiny.

Who's Who

Biblical Character	Claim to Fame
Adam	First human
Eve	Adam's wife
Able	Adam and Eve's godly son
Cain	Brother and murderer of Able
Noah	Built ship and with his family survived the great Flood
Abram	Later called Abraham, he was given the covenant promises
Sarai	Later called Sarah, she was Abraham's wife
Isaac	Son of Abraham and Sarah who inherited the promises
Ishmael	Son of Abraham and Sarah's maid; ancestor of the Arabs
Jacob	Also called Israel, he and his twelve sons inherited the promises and fatherhood of the Jewish people
Joseph	Victim of his brothers' jealousy whom God used to save family from famine

Exodus—The Story Continues

When we pick up the story from Genesis, the descendants of Abraham are enslaved in Egypt. Initially welcomed as guests, the family of some seventy men and women multiplied until their Egyptian hosts felt threatened by their numbers. The Egyptian answer: Work them to death! Make them kill their own newborn sons by throwing them into the Nile! So Exodus poses a question. Can the God who made a covenant promising blessings to Abraham's offspring deliver those blessings? And will he?

A Man and His Mission

Deliverance came in unlikely form. An Israelite child was adopted into Egypt's royal family. As an adult he identified with God's people. When he murdered an overseer who was mistreating an Israelite, he fled into the wilderness. He lived there, this one-time prince, herding sheep for forty years. Then, all ambition drained by the desert sun, God spoke to him out of a burning bush, announcing that he, Moses, had been chosen to deliver God's people.

God equipped Moses with two powerful resources. First, God revealed his personal name, a name that means "The One Who Is Always Present." Wherever "LORD" appears in our English Bibles, that personal name is found in the original text. Second, God gave Moses the power to perform miracles.

We are familiar with what happened when Moses confronted Egypt's pharaoh. That ruler scoffed. Egypt

The LORD said, "I have surely seen the affliction of My people who are in Egypt. . . . I am aware of their sufferings. So I have come down to deliver them."

Exodus 3:7–8 NASB

The Egyptians shall know that I am the LORD, when I stretch out My hand on Egypt and bring out the sons of Israel.

Exodus 7:5 NASB

was the world's greatest nation, her wealth and power ascribed to her gods and goddesses. Why would Pharaoh tremble before a god of slaves? But Moses initiated a series of devastating plagues that turned Egypt into a wasteland (Exodus 7–12). A humbled Pharaoh urged Moses to take God's people and leave, and God instituted Passover as a memorial celebration (Exodus 12).

On the Road

Moses led the throng of freed slaves out into the wilderness, where joy at their release quickly turned to complaint. Still God provided for their needs, and a miracle cloud led them to the base of Mount Sinai. There, as the mountaintop was obscured by roiling clouds and bolts of lightning, Moses met with God and was given a law for his people to live by.

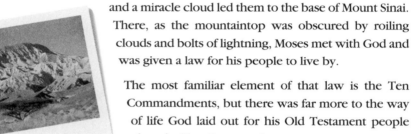

The most familiar element of that law is the Ten Commandments, but there was far more to the way of life God laid out for his Old Testament people than the Ten Commandments.

Elements of the Law

The Ten Commandments (Exodus 20). Ten principles that defined how to maintain healthy relationships with God and with other people were laid down. Those who followed these guidelines were promised long and blessed lives.

Case Law (Exodus 20–23). Specific cases were cited as examples of how the ten principles might be applied.

Worship Center (Exodus 25–27). Detailed instructions were given for the construction of a worship tent (tabernacle) where God would meet with his people. Each detail was significant, representing truths about the nature of relationship with God.

Priesthood (Exodus 28–30). Despite the fact that the freed slaves had committed themselves to obey the Law, God had no illusions. They would fail, and new priests would be needed to offer sacrifices to cover their sins and restore their fellowship with God.

The Fatal Flaw Revealed

While Moses was again on the mountain speaking with God, the people urged Aaron, Moses' brother, to fashion an idol (Exodus 31-33). Their promise to worship God was broken almost as soon as it was made. God had been faithful; Israel had not. And construction of the tabernacle was begun immediately (Exodus 34-40).

The Significance of the Book of Exodus

Exodus makes a vital contribution to our knowledge of God and of human nature. God kept his promises, and his miracles demonstrated his ability to act in our world of space and time. And the revelation of his name, often translated as "I AM," constitutes a wonderful reminder. Whatever the situation, God is always present with us. As for human nature, our essential flaw is seen in the complaints and ingratitude of a people freed from slavery and in their easy abandonment of God in favor of an idol.

> You shall serve the LORD your God, and He will bless.
>
> Exodus 23:25 NKJV

The Ten Commandments

Relationship with God	Relationships with Others
1. No gods before me.	5. Honor mother and father.
2. No idols.	6. Do not murder.
3. Do not deny my reality.	7. Do not commit adultery.
4. Keep the Sabbath holy.	8. Do not steal.
	9. Do not give false testimony.
	10. Do not covet.

Digging Deeper

 In Egypt Pharaoh was considered a minor deity, responsible for maintaining relationships with the major gods on whose favor Egypt's prosperity depended. The plagues showed up Egypt's deities as powerless fictions when God turned the Nile to blood, destroyed crops, and blotted out the light of the sun.

Must-Reads in Exodus

Several significant events are recorded in the book of Exodus. These events are listed in the chart below.

Situation/Event	Scripture
Condition of the slaves	Exodus 1–2
Moses reluctantly agrees to go	Exodus 3–4
Plagues ruin Egypt	Exodus 7–11
Moses parts Red Sea	Exodus 13–15
Ten Commandments	Exodus 20
Golden Calf	Exodus 32

Leviticus—Camped at Sinai

The Israelites remained at Mount Sinai while God was giving Moses detailed instructions concerning worship and lifestyle. Key words in this book are *holy* (eighty-seven times), *sacrifice* or *offerings* (more than three hundred times), and *atonement* (forty-nine times). The detailed rules patterned the lives of priests and people. The rules may seem strange to us, but they established a unique way of life that reminded the Israelites that they belonged to God, who won their release from slavery.

First Things First

The first ten chapters of Leviticus describe the sacrifices to be brought to the tabernacle worship center. Some sacrifices made atonement for sin; others were offerings that expressed thanks and joy in God's presence. Only descendants of Aaron could serve as priests and officiate at the sacrifices.

Don't live like the people of Egypt where you used to live, and don't live like the people of Canaan where I'm bringing you. Don't do what they do.

Leviticus 18:3 MSG

Set yourselves apart to be holy, for I am the LORD your God.

Leviticus 20:7 NLT

Ritual Do's and Don'ts

Chapters 11–15 contain rules about what can be eaten, infectious skin disease, and so forth. Violating these rules temporarily made a person ritually unclean (disqualified from approaching God in worship). Some people argue that concern for public health lay behind ritual regulations. It is best to understand them as constant reminders that the Israelites were a distinct people, marked by their relationship with God.

The Day of Atonement and Holiness

The Day of Atonement lies at the heart of this book and its message (chapters 16-17). Only a blood sacrifice offered by the high priest could cover the intentional sins of God's people, even as only the sacrifice of Jesus on Calvary could win forgiveness of our sins.

Chapters 18-22 focus on moral issues, appropriate punishments, and how priests and people were to show respect for the sacrifices and offering the Law commanded.

Celebration

Chapter 23 lays out the religious calendar; a calendar that called for joyous celebrations. The book concludes by addressing specific issues, including social mechanisms for relieving poverty (chapter 25).

Final Thoughts

Commitment to the distinctive way of life laid out here and in the other books of the Pentateuch has been a major factor in preserving the Jews as a distinct people for some thirty-four hundred years. While other ancient people were assimilated, the Jewish people have retained their unique identity over the millennia.

Key Terms in Leviticus

Holy	Commitment to God, as shown by obedience to his laws
Sin	Intentional or unintentional violation of God's law
Guilt	Liability to punishment for violation of God's law
Sacrifice	Offering of the blood of an animal as an atonement for sin
Atonement	Covering for sin that makes fellowship with God possible

Numbers—On the Road Again

Moses organized the camp and established a marching order. Led by a miraculous fiery cloud, the people set out from Sinai for the Promised Land. But despite the wonders they had witnessed, the Israelites failed to trust God. Poised on the border of Canaan, the people refused to enter. They were condemned to forty years of wandering in the wilderness. Decades later, a new generation did trust God, and they fought for the land promised to their forefathers.

Wasted Years

As Moses tells the story of the journey, three themes are emphasized. First, despite all God had done for the people he had saved from slavery, they remained ungrateful and rebellious. They failed to respond to God's discipline. This theme culminated in the open defiance of God's command to enter Canaan, a choice that doomed the first generation of Israelites to wander in the wilderness until every adult who left Egypt had died (chapters 13–14).

> All these men who have seen My glory and the signs which I did in Egypt and in the wilderness, and have put Me to the test now these ten times, and have not heeded My voice, they certainly shall not see the land.
>
> Numbers 14:22–23 NKJV

> You shall take possession of the land and live in it, for I have given the land to you to possess it.
>
> Numbers 33:53 NASB

The second theme is the faithfulness of God to his fractious people. Lack of faith might have doomed the first generation, but God's commitment remained unshaken. He kept his promises and brought their sons and daughters into Canaan. This theme is summed up in the story of Balaam, a wizard hired by the Moabites to curse Israel but who was moved by God to bless Israel instead (chapters 22–24).

The third theme traces the experiences of the new generation of Israelites, a generation that does trust and obey God. A census of the new generation (chapter 26), like one taken earlier at Sinai (chapter 1), showed Israel's military strength undiminished at some six hundred thousand men and marked the transition. As the new generation of Israelites moved purposefully toward the land promised them by God, they won a series of military victories. Moses provided fresh instructions they were to follow when the Promised Land was theirs (chapters 28–36).

Myth Buster

 In the early twentieth century, travelers wondered at the Bible's description of Canaan as "a land of milk and honey" because much of the land was dry and desolate. Yet this was a truly rich land in Bible times. The plains along the Mediterranean were well watered and fertile. The hills were wooded and green, and wildflowers dotted the mountain valleys. Today, as more land is irrigated and trees are planted, we are beginning to see Canaan's ancient beauty restored.

Digging Deeper

A census of some six hundred thousand men of military age (Numbers 26) suggests that the Israelites who left Egypt and traveled to Canaan may have numbered as many as 2.5 million!

Deuteronomy—Poised on Canaan's Border

The forty years of wandering in the wilderness ended. A new generation of Israelites waited beyond Canaan's borders to enter the Promised Land. Before they could, however, Moses died. But the great lawgiver performed a final duty. Before he died, Moses delivered a series of sermons that took the form of a Hittite *suzerainty* treaty: a formal constitution spelling out the relationship between a ruler and his people.

✻

God and the Israelites

The treaty format adopted by Moses helps us understand something special about the relationship between God and the Israelites. In ancient times, both rulers and people had obligations. The ruler committed himself to protect his people and to see to their well-being. The people committed themselves to be good citizens, to obey the ruler, and to abide by the laws that he laid down.

> You must love the LORD your God with all your heart, all your soul, and all your strength.
>
> Deuteronomy 6:5 NLT
>
> God-devotion makes a country strong; God-avoidance leaves people weak.
>
> Proverbs 14:34 MSG

As well as spelling out the obligations of ruler and people, the treaty—which we'd probably call a *constitution* today—spelled out the consequences should the people rebel against the ruler. In this case, the ruler was justified in punishing his people, even as he was obligated to see to their well-being should they be obedient to his laws.

Highlights in Deuteronomy

The treaty outline serves as an essential reading guide for Deuteronomy, one of the Old Testament's most significant books. No other

Old Testament book is as often quoted in the New Testament. According to Matthew 4, Jesus relied on principles stated in Deuteronomy to overcome Satan's temptations. But what is most special is that Deuteronomy set up the primacy of love in moving God to establish this relationship with his people, and it set up the necessity of a love motivation for Israel to keep her treaty with God.

Tragically, Israel was destined to violate the treaty repeatedly, and so the curses of Deuteronomy 28:15–68 serve as an unhappy preview of Israel's future. Later prophets looked back on this passage to explain tragedies that befell their contemporaries and to fix responsibility for the nation's troubles squarely on a spiritually depraved or indifferent people.

Final Thoughts

Today's nations are not ancient Israel, nor do modern nations have a similar claim on God's favor. At the same time, the moral principles imbedded in Moses' law do state lasting standards of behavior that apply to all peoples. Now as then, violating these standards has consequences.

Digging Deeper

The Hebrew word translated *Law (torah)* means "teaching." It is broadly applied to the five books of Moses as well as to the Ten Commandments and the some six hundred–plus specific rules Jewish rabbis have identified in the Old Testament. These many rules shaped every facet of Israel's personal, civil, international, and religious activities, effectively setting God's people apart from other nations and peoples to this day.

The Books of History and Poetry

As the centuries rolled by, God's people lived on the land God promised them, sometimes prospering, sometimes waning. Their poetry expressed emotions and praise that probed the meaning of human life.

Contents

The Tragic Story of a Straying People 89

Joshua—Conquest of Canaan 91

Judges and Ruth—Plunge into Darkness 93

1 and 2 Samuel—The Age of Transition 97

1 and 2 Kings—Inevitable Decline 101

1 and 2 Chronicles—History in Divine Perspective 105

Ezra and Nehemiah—Exiles Return 107

Esther—Insight into Providence 111

The Practical Poets of Scripture 113

Job—Story of Triumph over Harsh Troubles 115

Psalms—Songs of Passion, Joy, and Awe 117

Proverbs—Pithy Principles of Right and Wrong 121

Ecclesiastes—Writings of Discernment and Knowledge ... 123

Song of Solomon—Collection of Love Poems 125

Sing for joy in the LORD, O you righteous ones;
praise is becoming to the upright.

Psalm 33:1 NASB

The Tragic Story of a Straying People

As we close Deuteronomy, we leave a confident people, equipped with a unique formal relationship with God and boundless confidence in him. That confidence was soon rewarded, and the people surged into Canaan to take possession of the Promised Land. But as generation succeeded generation, trust in God waxed and waned. The history of Israel from the conquest around 1390 BC to the fall of the remaining Hebrew kingdom in 587 BC demonstrates the faithfulness of God to his promise to bless—and to punish—as the law treaty requires.

A Thousand Years of Bible History: 1390–445 BC

The successful invasion of Palestine under Joshua didn't lead to the establishment of a united nation. For several hundred years, the Israelites struggled to maintain a foothold in the land. During these centuries, leaders called *judges* emerged. Finally the last of the judges, Samuel, appointed Saul as Israel's first king. Saul, who was flawed by his inability to rely on God, was replaced by David. David unified the Israelites and forged a powerful, united Hebrew kingdom. Upon David's death, his son Solomon ruled for forty years. But when Solomon died, the nation divided into northern and southern kingdoms.

They continually mocked the messengers of God, despised His words and scoffed at His prophets, until the wrath of the LORD arose against His people, until there was no remedy.

2 Chronicles 36:16 NASB

They put God to the test and rebelled against the Most High; they did not keep his statutes.

Psalm 78:56 NIV

The first ruler in the north, Jeroboam, feared that a common religion would lead to a reunification. He set up a counterfeit religion, mimicking elements of the religious system revealed to Moses. Every ruler in the north (Israel) continued this system. Israel finally fell to Assyria in 722, and its population was scattered throughout the Assyrian Empire.

In the south (Judah), an unbroken chain of King David's descendants ruled. While a number of these kings were godly, too many rejected God and his law. The southern kingdom survived until 586, when it was overrun by Babylon and Jerusalem was destroyed.

After some seventy years in Babylon, a small contingent of Jews intent on rebuilding the temple returned to the Holy Land. While the temple was rebuilt, the Holy Land remained under foreign control until the time of Jesus.

Final Thoughts

Exodus through Deuteronomy saw the establishment of a unique formal relationship (the law treaty) between God and Israel. Under that treaty blessings would flow if Israel was faithful to God. The books of history trace in tragic detail the story of a people who continually turned from God and suffered terrible consequences.

Check Your Understanding

- **What is the natural division within the five books of the Pentateuch, and what period of time do they cover?**

Genesis goes back to Creation and the covenant with Abraham. Events in the other four books take place within Moses' lifetime. Altogether they cover roughly a thousand years, from 1400 BC to 445 BC.

- **How do the books of history carry on the Bible's story?**

The books of history describe the efforts of the Israelites to abide by the law treaty. Their repeated failure validates Scripture's teaching that humans are flawed by sin. They also demonstrate God's commitment to his promises, both to reward and to punish.

Joshua—Conquest of Canaan

In a series of devastating strikes, the forces of Joshua, Moses' successor, penetrated Canaan's central highlands. They then swung south and north to defeat coalitions of Canaanite city-states. With the enemy forces crushed, Joshua divided the land by lot, assigning each Israelite tribe its own territory. The story of the conquest teaches an important lesson: obedience to God guarantees victory, as evidenced by God's personally granting each family its holdings.

Conquest highlights

Joshua's credentials as Moses' successor were quickly established when the river Jordan at flood stage parted to permit the Israelites to enter Canaan (chapters 1-4). There, blocking the way into the central highlands, stood the walled city of Jericho. The "battle" was the strangest ever fought, as the Israelites silently marched around the city for six days. Then on the seventh day the people shouted, and the city walls collapsed (chapters 5-6). The lesson learned is that God is one who provides victory. Israel's role was obedience, however strange God's commands may have seemed.

The LORD our God is He who brought us and our fathers up out of the land of Egypt. . . . We also will serve the LORD, for He is our God.

Joshua 24:17-18 NASB

If you abandon the LORD and serve other gods, he will turn against you and destroy you, even though he has been so good to you.

Joshua 24:20 NLT

The lesson was underlined when a soldier named Achan disobeyed God and secreted some of Jericho's wealth in his tent. This led to a defeat at Ai, and it established a corollary. As obedience brings victory, disobedience brings defeat (chapter 7).

The second half of Joshua (chapters 13–24) describes the distribution of the land to Israelite tribes and families by casting lots, which is similar to throwing dice. The tribe of Levi, which served as priests and was to teach God's Word, was given forty-eight cities scattered through the lands of the other tribes. Six "cities of refuge" were established where anyone who killed accidentally could flee until he or she had a fair trial. At last the Israelites were settled in the Promised Land, with God having kept every promise he made.

Final Thoughts

As the book ends, the Israelites have defeated the dominant city-states in Canaan and are firmly established in the land. But not all of the Canaanites were driven out. Joshua challenged the people to continue serving God. Joshua was all too aware that without God's help the Israelites were vulnerable.

Digging Deeper

Jericho's massive walls, some thirty-five feet high, rested on an eleven-foot sloped stone base. In harmony with the biblical account, the walls tumbled outward. Archaeologists debate the date of Jericho's fall, but recent pottery dating indicates a date of about 1400 BC.

Judges and Ruth—Plunge into Darkness

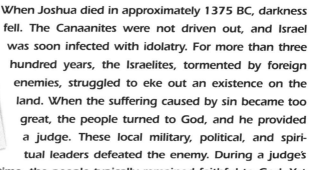

When Joshua died in approximately 1375 BC, darkness fell. The Canaanites were not driven out, and Israel was soon infected with idolatry. For more than three hundred years, the Israelites, tormented by foreign enemies, struggled to eke out an existence on the land. When the suffering caused by sin became too great, the people turned to God, and he provided a judge. These local military, political, and spiritual leaders defeated the enemy. During a judge's lifetime, the people typically remained faithful to God. Yet on the death of a judge the Israelites quickly strayed. The books of Judges and Ruth take us deep into this dark period of Israel's history.

Causes of the Plunge into Darkness

Judges 1:1–3:6 explains the causes of the plunge into darkness. Rather than obey God and drive out the remaining Canaanites, some of the Canaanites were permitted to remain. Some Israelite tribes even enslaved defeated enemies.

Sin, Servitude, Supplication, and Salvation

The most significant feature of the bulk of the book, Judges 3:7–16:31, is its description of a repeated pattern of behavior, a pattern Israel seemed unable to break. Each cycle began with *sin*, as the Israelites turned to idolatry and forgot God's law. Sin led to *servitude*, as foreign enemies oppressed the Israelites, raiding their land and taking their

> The people of Israel lived among the Canaanites. . . . Israelite sons married their daughters, and Israelite daughters were given in marriage to their sons. And the Israelites served their gods.
>
> Judges 3:5–6 NLT
>
> The Israelites stopped worshiping the LORD and worshiped the idols of Baal and Astarte, as well as the idols of other gods from nearby nations.
>
> Judges 2:11 CEV

harvests. Servitude in turn led to *supplication*, as the people appealed to God. God responded, providing *salvation* in the person of a judge. During the judge's lifetime the people remained faithful to God and thus were *secure*, but they quickly turned from God when the judge died. This cycle was repeated time after time.

The People God Used

The book identifies thirteen judges, four of whom are especially prominent: Deborah (Judges 4–5) was a woman and a prophet. The Bible says that she "led" Israel. In a patriarchal society like that of Israel, Deborah must have been an exceptional individual who engendered enough trust to rally troops to defeat the oppressing army. In fact, each of the four major judges seems to be an exception. Gideon (Judges 6–8) described himself as an insignificant man from an insignificant family. Yet God chose him to defeat a massive army from Midian. Jephath was an illegitimate son expelled from the family after his father's death (Judges 11:1–12:7). Samson (Judges 13–16), renowned for his physical strength, was morally weak and finally was betrayed to the Philistine enemy by a prostitute he frequented. How often God chooses to use people we would overlook!

Life in the Era of the Judges

The final five chapters of Judges and the little book of Ruth tell stories of ordinary individuals. Their stories reveal what life was like during what some have called Israel's dark age.

Micah's Idols (chapters 17–18). Micah stole silver from his mother. When she placed a curse on the thief, Micah was terrified and confessed. He then made a household idol from the silver and hired a Levite to serve as his priest. Every action described in this story was in unwitting violation of Moses' law: the mother's use of a curse, Micah's theft, the making of an idol, and the Levite serving as a priest, a role reserved for descendants of Aaron. The story brings home the general ignorance of God's law that prevailed in the era of the judges.

A Levite (chapter 19). The concubine (secondary wife) of a Levite ran away, and the Levite recovered her. On the way home, the Levite stayed overnight in an Israelite town. But the men of the town were bent on raping the visitor. The Levite, intent on saving himself, forced his concubine outside. The next morning the woman was found dead. The Levite, morally outraged, called for justice.

At that time there was no king in Israel. People did whatever they felt like doing.

Judges 21:25 MSG

The Levite was apparently unaware that his own actions were grossly immoral. Thus Judges reminds us that the lack of standards corrupts society.

Civil War (chapters 20–21). The tribes gathered to punish the men of the town where the Levite's concubine was killed, but the tribe of Dan chose to fight to protect their clansmen. In the civil war that followed, thousands were killed.

Ruth. Ruth was a Moabite married to a Jewish man. When her husband died, Ruth accompanied Naomi, her mother-in-law, who returned to Bethlehem in Israel. There Ruth's commitment to Naomi and her subsequent marriage to a godly man led to the birth of a child who became the great-grandfather of King David. This lovely story reminds us that even in the darkest of times ordinary people who honor God can experience his blessing.

Final Thoughts

Even in a society that is totally corrupt, there's hope for those who remain faithful to God. A nation may forget God, but God will never forget individuals who honor him. How important it is to read the Bible, the better to know God and to understand his will.

Digging Deeper

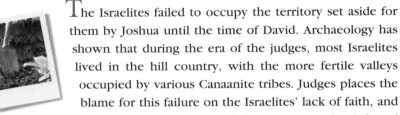

The Israelites failed to occupy the territory set aside for them by Joshua until the time of David. Archaeology has shown that during the era of the judges, most Israelites lived in the hill country, with the more fertile valleys occupied by various Canaanite tribes. Judges places the blame for this failure on the Israelites' lack of faith, and also on the practice of some tribal groups to make defeated Canaanites slaves rather than to drive them from the land. This proved disastrous, as it led to intermarriage among the people of the land and to Israel's adoption of many false religious concepts, idolatry, and immorality. It was not until after the Babylonian captivity a thousand years later that the Israelite religion was purged of idolatry.

Myth Buster

Ruth's marriage illustrates the role of "kinsman-redeemer." Only a near relation has a right to restore another's lost family and possessions. Only by becoming human could God call us to a union with him that restores our lost innocence.

"Naomi said, 'Where did you work today? Whose field was it? God bless the man who treated you so well!' Then Ruth told her that she had worked in the field of a man named Boaz. 'The Lord bless Boaz!' Naomi replied. 'He has shown that he is still loyal to the living and to the dead. Boaz is a close relative, one of those who is supposed to look after us'" (Ruth 2:19–20 CEV).

1 and 2 Samuel—The Age of Transition

The two books of Samuel tell the story of three figures who mark the transition from the days judges ruled disorganized tribes to the emergence of a united Israel as a dominant power in the Middle East. The three figures are Samuel, the last of the judges; Saul, Israel's first king; and David, the military and organizational genius who in just forty years welded the tribes into one and expanded Israeli-controlled territory some ten times over. These books, along with 1 Chronicles, focus on the transition years (1050 BC to 970 BC) as the aged Samuel reluctantly anointed Israel's first and second kings.

Samuel (1 Samuel 1–8)

The last and greatest of the judges was born about 1100 BC. As a child, Samuel was dedicated to serve God. He grew up to lead the struggle of the Israelites against the Philistines, Israel's primary enemy at the time. Although the Israelites won a military victory, Philistine control of ironworking technology kept the tribes dependent. When Samuel grew old, the Israelites demanded he appoint a king. Samuel recognized this demand as a rejection of God's rule, but he reluctantly gave in.

> Because you said No to God's command, he says No to your kingship.
>
> 1 Samuel 15:23 MSG
>
> Man does not see what the LORD sees, for man sees what is visible, but the LORD sees the heart.
>
> 1 Samuel 16:7 HCSB

Saul (1 Samuel 9–31)

God directed Samuel to a young man named Saul. Although an unknown from a minor tribe and family, Saul was the tallest and strongest of the Israelites. When the young king won a victory over an Ammonite force, his authority was established. But the Philistines saw the new Israelite monarchy as a threat, and they assembled a massive army to kill Saul. The young king panicked and disobeyed God, revealing a fatal flaw in Saul's character. Saul's forty-two-year reign was marked by additional failures and sins. Saul and his sons were killed in a last battle with the Philistines.

David (1 Samuel 16–31; 2 Samuel; 2 Chronicles)

God sent Samuel to anoint an unknown teen named David as the next king of Israel. David became a national hero when he killed the giant Goliath in one-on-one combat. David quickly demonstrated a genius for military leadership, awakening a fierce jealousy in Saul. When Saul tried to murder his rival, David became an outlaw. After Saul's death, David was acclaimed king by the tribe of Judah. Seven years later, about 1003 BC, David was finally acclaimed king of all the tribes, and ruled until his death in 970 BC.

The following accomplishments are credited to David:

- Israel was firmly established as a monarchy.

- The loose confederation of tribes became a united nation.

- Anarchy was replaced by a strong central government.

- The people moved from bronze-age poverty to a strong iron-age economy.

- The Israelites who had lived as a subject people became conquerors.

- Local worship centers were replaced by a single worship center in Jerusalem, making it both the religious and political capital of the nation.

The Big Picture

The Bible's overarching story of how God intended to deal with human sin and restore relationship with him is carried forward in these books. A promise made to David is recorded in 2 Samuel 7: At history's end, one of his descendants would rule as king over the nation of Israel and the entire world. This expectation is woven through the rest of the Old Testament. God intended to accomplish his purposes through the nation of Israel and through a promised king. This promise, known as the Davidic covenant, prepares us to see Jesus, a descendant of David, as the King and Savior destined to accomplish all God's purposes when he returns.

An Assessment of David

An unmatched war leader, David defeated all Israel's enemies. A gifted administrator, David established efficient government, tax, worship, and military structures. His impact on Israel's worship is reflected in the psalms he wrote and the rituals he established (2 Chronicles 29). Although praised as a man whose heart was in tune with God (1 Kings 2:33; 3:6), the Bible never glosses over the sins he committed during his reign (2 Samuel 11–12, 24). What distinguished David from Saul was his readiness to confess his faults publicly and to seek forgiveness. David is also an important figure in the New Testament, but there the focus is on Jesus. The New Testament carefully traces Jesus' line back to David (Luke 2), teaching that the covenant promises God made to David were to be fulfilled in Jesus.

> Your house and your kingdom shall endure before Me forever; your throne shall be established forever.
>
> 2 Samuel 7:16 NASB

Digging Deeper

The city of Jerusalem rested on the border between the northern and southern Israelite tribes. David captured the city, and made it the political and religious capital of his kingdom. The site was rich in religious tradition: Abraham offered to sacrifice his son Isaac where the Jerusalem temple was erected.

Many tales are woven in and out as the main theme of the Bible's story develops. In the chart below are a few of these fascinating tales, stories from Saul's and David's lives.

Myth Buster

Scholars once treated the stories of Saul and David as mythic tales. But archaeological excavations have shown that details of the stories accurately reflect local conditions. For instance, 1 Samuel portrays Saul's armies without iron weapons, a significant reason for Philistine military superiority. Now archaeological digs have demonstrated that before 1000 BC, only areas occupied by the Philistines contained iron tools or weapons. Today, too, the date of Solomon's reign has been firmly established, as have the building projects ascribed to Solomon in the Bible. The biblical account has been shown to be historically accurate.

Rich Insights for Life Today

Theme	Scripture
A good start	1 Samuel 11
Saul's flaw	1 Samuel 13
Saul rejected	1 Samuel 15
David and Goliath	1 Samuel 17
Jealousy	1 Samuel 18
Out of control	1 Samuel 22
David and Abigail	1 Samuel 25
David spares Saul	1 Samuel 26
A bitter end	1 Samuel 28
David's prayer	2 Samuel 7:18–29
David's sin	2 Samuel 11–12
David's confession	Psalm 51

1 and 2 Kings—Inevitable Decline

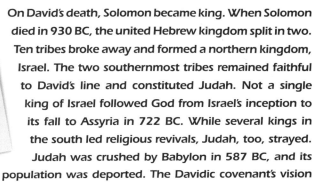

On David's death, Solomon became king. When Solomon died in 930 BC, the united Hebrew kingdom split in two. Ten tribes broke away and formed a northern kingdom, Israel. The two southernmost tribes remained faithful to David's line and constituted Judah. Not a single king of Israel followed God from Israel's inception to its fall to Assyria in 722 BC. While several kings in the south led religious revivals, Judah, too, strayed. Judah was crushed by Babylon in 587 BC, and its population was deported. The Davidic covenant's vision of an eternal Hebrew kingdom ruled by a descendant of David seemed impossible.

✳

Solomon's United Kingdom (1 Kings 1–11)

Solomon, David's son, ruled forty years. He relied on diplomacy, trade, and a strong army to maintain peace. Solomon was the wisest man of his time. In addition to studies of animal and plant life, Solomon wrote many proverbs. He is credited with authorship of two of the Bible's poetic books. Under Solomon, Israel became wealthy, but the king's many building projects required heavy taxes. He entered many marriages to solidify treaties with foreign nations. This was a mistake. In his later years his wives induced him to worship their deities, and he strayed from God.

All of this happened because the people of Israel had sinned against the LORD their God, who had rescued them from Egypt, where they had been slaves.

2 Kings 17:7 CEV

They poked fun at God's messengers, despised the message itself, and in general treated the prophets like idiots. GOD became more and more angry until there was no turning back.

2 Chronicles 36:16 MSG

Israel

Jeroboam, the first king of Israel, had a problem. Moses' law required that God's people worship at the central temple several times each year. Jeroboam feared this tie to Jerusalem, the capital of Judah, would lead to reunification. His first act as king was to establish a counterfeit religion for Israel with its own holidays and priests and religious centers. Israel supposedly would continue to worship God, but in ways that violated his law. Many from the north moved to Judah rather than participate in Jeroboam's religion. But succeeding kings of Israel maintained this counterfeit religion. Under a series of increasingly evil kings, Israel experienced a precipitous spiritual and moral decline that led to invasion by Sargon II in 722 BC and the resettlement of Israel's citizens throughout the vast Assyrian Empire.

A clear impression of the kings of Israel can be gained by reading about the first king, Jeroboam (1 Kings 12–13), and about the nation's most wicked king, Ahab (1 Kings 18; 20–21).

Judah

The southern kingdom had its share of evil rulers. But eight of Judah's nineteen kings are identified in the Bible as "good." Four led religious revivals. A revival under King Hezekiah led to the withdrawal of an invading Assyrian army, and the southern kingdom survived for another 135 years. Despite the influence of godly kings, Judah, too, was in spiritual decline. People turned to pagan ways and deities. The fifty-five-year reign of Hezekiah's wicked son, Manasseh, set Judah on a course that could not be reversed. In a final invasion, the Babylonians under Nebuchadnezzar destroyed Jerusalem and its temple and deported the population to Babylon.

Insight into biblical revivals is provided in 2 Kings 18–19, which also tells the story of the failed Assyrian invasion, while 2 Kings 21 gives a sketch of Manasseh's reign.

Revivals in Judah

A *revival* is a widespread rededication to God and his commandments. The four revivals recorded in 1 and 2 Kings have several things in common: (1) Each was initiated by the personal commitment of one of Judah's kings to God. (2) Each involved the purging of everything that competed for the people's religious allegiance. (3) Each incorporated the purification and restoration of temple worship. (4) The greatest revivals were stimulated and guided by the Bible. These kings led revivals in Judah:

> The remnant will return, the remnant of Jacob, to the Mighty God.
>
> Isaiah 10:21 NKJV

Asa (910-869 BC). Asa repaired the Jerusalem temple and attempted to stamp out idolatry in Judah. Many moved from Israel to Judah (1 Kings 15:9-24).

Jehoshaphat (872-848 BC). In Israel, Ahab attempted to eradicate worship of God. In Judah, Jehoshaphat removed local shrines and sent out Levites to teach the Bible (1 Kings 22:41-50; 2 Chronicles 18-20).

Hezekiah (715-686 BC). Hezekiah reopened the closed temple and restored the religious festivals commanded in Moses' law. He also tried to remove "high places" where idols were worshiped (2 Kings 18-20).

Josiah (640-609 BC). Guided by recovered lost books of Scripture, Josiah zealously attacked idolatry, destroying pagan altars and worship centers. He restored temple worship and reinstituted Passover and other worship festivals.

Prophets

While 1 and 2 Kings focus on the rulers of the two Hebrew kingdoms, prophets played significant roles in their stories. Prophets were spokespersons who delivered special messages and guidance from God.

Final Thoughts

The fall of Israel and Judah seems to have frustrated God's purposes as stated in the Davidic covenant. In fact, their fall confirms God's commitment to Scripture, for God imposed the very punishments threatened in Deuteronomy 28:15–68! People may miss God's blessing, but we can never thwart God's purposes.

Digging Deeper

Archaeologists have excavated a number of Solomon's building projects. The best known is Megiddo, a fortress city that controlled two trade routes. Building techniques used there, including the "double entry" gate, have enabled scholars to identify other ruins as dating from Solomon's era.

Myth Buster

Critics often object to the suggestion that God used an evil spirit to deceive King Ahab (1 Kings 22). Read the story carefully, however. The false prophets were the ones who were influenced by the evil spirit. God revealed the truth through Micaiah, a known prophet of the Lord. Where lies abound, God reveals the truth. We, like Ahab, are then responsible for which we will choose.

1 and 2 Chronicles—History in Divine Perspective

The Chronicles cover the period described in 2 Samuel and 1 and 2 Kings. Tradition identifies the author as Ezra, who wrote to encourage the exiles who returned to the Jewish homeland in 538 BC. The focus is worship. The theme is that when God's people were faithful, as demonstrated by commitment to temple worship, the nation prospered. The theme is developed through accounts of David's and Solomon's commitment to worship and analyses of the role temple worship played in Judah's revivals. The implicit message is that if the returned exiles give worship its proper place, God will bless and the future will be bright.

Significance of the Temple

The temple that Solomon constructed (1 Kings 5-8) played a central role in Hebrew religion. It was the one place where Israelites could meet with God, and it was a visible symbol of his presence. Only at the Jerusalem temple could the sacrifices be offered that covered an Israelite's sin and made fellowship with God possible. Every religious revival included a restoration of temple worship. In the end, the people of Judah mistook the symbol for reality and assumed the temple's mere presence guaranteed Jerusalem's safety. In fact, the sins of the people finally caused God to withdraw his presence from the temple (Ezekiel 8-11) before it was destroyed in 587 BC.

This is the temple where you have chosen to be worshiped. Please watch over it day and night and listen when I turn toward it and pray. . . . Whenever any of us look toward this temple and pray, answer from your home in heaven and forgive our sins.

2 Chronicles 6:20–21 CEV

Within your temple, O God, we meditate on your unfailing love.

Psalm 48:9 NIV

Three Temples

The Bible tells of three temples. The first was built by Solomon and destroyed by the Babylonians. The second was completed in 516 BC by the exiles who returned to Judah, and it was greatly expanded by Herod the Great in the first century. The second temple was destroyed in AD 70. The prophet Ezekiel (Ezekiel 40–48) described a yet-future third temple, associated with the rule of the Messiah.

Digging Deeper

The temple was constructed on the same plan as the worship tent (tabernacle) of Moses' time. Each featured a courtyard with a single entrance. An altar for sacrifice stood directly inside the entrance. Within the structure itself was an inner room that could be accessed only by the high priest once a year. The symbolism of only one way to God, that of blood sacrifice, and an inner sanctuary, too holy for ordinary persons to enter, is later developed and explained in the New Testament book of Hebrews.

Theological Overview

Overview	Scripture
Genealogies show that sacred history leads up to David.	1 Chronicles 1–10
David, Judah's greatest king, was a worshiper of God.	1 Chronicles 11–16
David served God by designing the temple and the worship to take place there.	1 Chronicles 17–29
Solomon, who built the temple, achieved great things.	2 Chronicles 1–9
Throughout Judah's history, the nation prospered when rulers led the nation to emphasize worship.	2 Chronicles 10–36

Ezra and Nehemiah—Exiles Return

After seventy years in Babylon, some forty-two thousand Jews were given permission to return to their devastated homeland. Their intent was to rebuild the temple; their first act was to lay its foundations. But the struggle to wrest a living from land overgrown with thorns, amid hostile neighbors, drained the Jews' resolve. It was eighteen years before the temple was completed, and many more years under the leadership of men like Ezra and Nehemiah until the city of Jerusalem was rebuilt and repopulated. Even then, the little Jewish colony existed only as a minor district in one of the many provinces of the mighty Persian Empire.

The Setting

Jeremiah had predicted that the Babylonian captivity would last seventy years (Jeremiah 25:1–14; 29:10). Reckoning from the first deportation in 605 BC, the seventieth year is 536 BC. In 538 BC, Cyrus the Great of Persia overthrew Babylon and established the Persian Empire. That same year he reversed Babylon's policy and allowed conquered peoples to return to their homelands. Cyrus encouraged them to worship their national deities and to pray for him.

The Jews had prospered in Babylon, and most of them were comfortable there. Only a few chose to return to the Promised Land, moved primarily by a desire to rebuild their temple and worship God in ways Scripture decrees. The first group of Jews arrived home in 536 BC.

Ezra had spent his entire life studying and obeying the Law of the LORD and teaching it to others.

Ezra 7:10 CEV

In those days I also saw Jews who had married women of Ashdod, Ammon, and Moab. . . . So I contended with them and cursed them, struck some of them and pulled out their hair, and made them swear by God.

Nehemiah 13:23, 25 NKJV

The Book of Ezra

Ezra 1–6 tells the story of the early years. The returnees settled in small villages outside Jerusalem, but they set up an altar and laid the foundation of a new temple on the site of the first. Neighboring peoples, who were resettled in the northern kingdom by Assyria some three hundred years earlier, were hostile. They forced work on the temple to stop. Eighteen years later the prophets Haggai and Zechariah rekindled the Jews' zeal, and the temple was completed. But it took a decree of the current emperor to curb the neighbors' opposition.

Ezra 7–10 picks up the story some fifty-eight years later in 457 BC. A student of Scripture, Ezra the Scribe was moved to lead another party back to Jerusalem from Babylon. He arrived with a royal commission to appoint judges and enforce both God's law and Persian law in Judea. Ezra was shocked to find the people had begun to intermarry with pagan neighbors and had grown lax about keeping the Law. Under his teaching, the people made a fresh commitment to serve God.

The Book of Nehemiah

Nehemiah 1–7 introduces Nehemiah, who arrived in Jerusalem in 444 BC, a hundred years after the first group of exiles returned. Nehemiah was a high court official who begged to be appointed governor of Jerusalem, an insignificant splinter of the Persian Empire, in order to rebuild the city walls. In ancient times, only walled cities were deemed significant, and Nehemiah could not bear the thought of Jerusalem's humiliation.

Nehemiah rallied the people. Despite threats from the neighboring peoples and internal dissension, the Jews rebuilt the city walls in record time.

Nehemiah 8–12 reveals continuing indifference to God's law. But Ezra's public prayer of confession stimulated a revival, and an agreement to end violation of the Law was signed by the leading Jews. Nehemiah moved a tenth of the Jewish population into Jerusalem, and the new walls were dedicated.

Nehemiah 13 ends the books of history on a note of uncertainty. Nehemiah left Judea briefly to report to the king. When he returned he was shocked to find temple worship abandoned, more intermarriage with pagans, and the Sabbath being violated. God's people had slid into sin so quickly with Nehemiah gone! What was to become of the Jews in the future?

Impact of the Captivity

The years in Babylon had a significant impact on the Jews and their religion. Before the captivity, the Israelites were susceptible to idolatry. The captivity purged them of this vulnerability. In Babylon, without a temple as their faith's focus, the Jews turned to the Scriptures. The synagogue as a local place of worship and study grew out of men's meetings in Babylon to explore the Word of God. Men like Ezra,

> Tell the godly that all will be well for them. They will enjoy the rich reward they have earned!
>
> Isaiah 3:10 NLT

who committed himself to master the Scriptures, became the rabbis, the teachers of the Law we read of in the New Testament, and later the sages, who codified Jewish belief and practice in the first and second centuries AD. The captivity, which at the time must have seemed a disaster, was transformed into a blessing, becoming the stimulant for a movement that is a primary cause of the preservation of God's Old Testament people to this day.

Final Thoughts

The God who knows the end from the beginning has the future firmly in his control. We see that clearly when we look at the many prophecies focusing on the birth, life, and death of Jesus. Fulfilled prophecy assures us that when history does draw to a close, all God's purposes will be fulfilled.

Digging Deeper

Old Testament covenants and prophecies portray a restored nation of Israel in the land given her by God. This is invariably the setting for images of events to take place at history's end. Yet from Jerusalem's fall in 587 BC to the twentieth century, no such Jewish state existed. Then in 1948 a Jewish state came into existence. It is no wonder many students of the Bible see 1948 as pivotal, a portent of the return of Jesus. Still, God's purposes and God's timing remain a mystery. We can never say with certainty how long history stretches out before us.

Bible Links

We're used to links on the Internet: easy jumps to additional information. The Bible has its own links, and following the links is a great way to enhance knowledge of the Bible. For instance, the book of Ezra is closely linked to the prophetic books of Haggai and Zechariah. Each prophet urged the Jews to rebuild the temple. Check Haggai, and you will receive insight into conditions twenty years into the recolonization of Judea. Check Zechariah, and you will see how Scripture deals with the prospect of centuries of Gentile domination of the Jewish homeland. Nehemiah is closely linked with Malachi, the last book of the Old Testament. We sense Nehemiah's frustration with an indifferent people in chapter 13, and Malachi reveals how that indifference to God deepened after Nehemiah's governorship. Enrich your understanding of Scripture by checking the links between books of the Bible.

Esther—Insight into Providence

The story is set in Susa, then capital of the Persian Empire. Esther was a young Jewish girl who unexpectedly became queen. About the same time, a high royal official determined to avenge an insult by wiping out the Jewish people. Through a series of "coincidences," Esther found herself in a position to thwart the plot, but at great personal risk. Bravely Esther went to her royal husband, and as coincidence piled upon coincidence, the Jewish people were saved. Today the Jewish Festival of Purim continues to celebrate Esther and the deliverance of the Jewish people.

Esther's Peculiarities

The events in Esther probably took place midway through the reign of the Persian king Xerxes (485–464 BC). Xerxes tried to invade Greece, but the Athenians and their allies defeated him twice, thus saving the budding democracies. It is likely the great banquet described in chapter 1 was a gathering held to plan the second invasion of Europe.

> Who knows? Maybe you were made queen for just such a time as this.
>
> Esther 4:14 MSG
>
> The lot is cast into the lap, but its every decision is from the LORD.
>
> Proverbs 16:33 NKJV

The most peculiar thing about the book of Esther is that there is no mention of God in the entire book. Yet as coincidence piles upon coincidence, it becomes utterly clear that God is behind the scenes, directing events in such a way as to preserve his people. For instance, Haman, the bitter enemy of the Jews, cast lots for months waiting for a propitious moment to strike. Finally, the omens favored Haman. But that night the king could not sleep. He had servants read the archives, and he discovered that the Jew Haman hated had once saved the king's life. The tables were turned, and when Queen Esther revealed that she was a Jew, Haman suffered the fate he intended for his enemies.

More than any other book in the Old Testament, Esther reads like a novel, packed with tension and plot twists. It is a book to read and enjoy rather than study, at least to simply read *before* studying. Esther is fun reading. At the same time, its message is clear. God does not need miracles to manage the events of this world, or to keep his people safe.

Final Thoughts

One place to look for the hand of God is in the circumstances of our daily lives. Seemingly random events do seem to come together to shape the direction of our lives. Look with faith, and you may see the hand of God where others see chance.

Digging Deeper

Providence can be defined as "the continuous active involvement of God in the created universe, shaping events according to his purposes." We might call providence the hidden hand of God in events that shape our lives. The notion that God is constantly at work in and through circumstances is uniquely biblical. It depends  on (1) the conviction that God is all-powerful and (2) that God has a loving concern for human beings. It is important to note that Providence doesn't cancel free will. We humans still choose how we respond to our circumstances. But it is comforting to contemplate the events described in Esther, and to then look back and marvel at how God has worked in our lives.

The Practical Poets of Scripture

Open one of the Bible's poetic books, and, at first glance, it doesn't read like poetry at all. There is no moon in June, no rain in Spain that stays on the plain. Bible poetry simply doesn't rhyme. Even the subject matter seems strange. Job and three friends philosophize about suffering. The writer of Ecclesiastes mopes over life's meaning, and Solomon tosses out one-liners in Proverbs. At least the Song of Solomon reads like a love poem. And Psalms, well, worship hymns fit, maybe. But overall, the poetic books of the Bible don't look like poetry, and their content is, well, different.

Understanding Hebrew Poetry

Unlike our poetry, Hebrew poetry isn't based on rhyme. It is based on putting ideas together in three basic patterns. The patterns develop a thought by adding a line that is synonymous, adding a line that's opposite, or adding several lines that enrich the idea stated at the first. These patterns are called *synonymous parallelism, antithetical parallelism,* and *synthetic parallelism*. It's the way thoughts are developed that marks Hebrew poetry.

Take synonymous parallelism. The first idea is developed by saying the same thing in a different way. Psalm 126:2 reports: "Our mouths were filled with laughter, our tongues with songs of joy" (NIV).

> Listen to counsel and accept discipline, that you may be wise the rest of your days.
>
> Proverbs 19:20 NASB
>
> Praise the LORD, all you nations. Praise him, all you people of the earth.
>
> Psalm 117:1 NLT

Antithetical parallelism takes an opposites approach, as in Proverbs 11:17: "A kind man benefits himself, but a cruel man brings trouble on himself" (NIV).

And, as noted, synthetic parallelism stacks idea upon idea to build a clear impression, as in Psalm 1:3: "He is like a tree planted by streams of water, which yields its fruit in season and whose leaf does not wither" (NIV).

Advantages of Hebrew poetry

Unlike rhyming poetry, Hebrew poetry can be translated into any language. And unlike our poetry, Hebrew poetry is adapted to almost any kind of literature, from philosophical discourse to how-to. That's why the Bible's poetic books are so diverse in subject matter. Hebrew poetry is ideal for exploring and examining ideas, as well as for expressing emotions and, especially, for expressing praise.

Final Thoughts

In reading the poetic books, or many passages in the Prophets, be aware of how Hebrew poetry works. Recognizing the parallelism patterns will enrich your reading.

Check Your Understanding

- **What kinds of biblical literature are presented in poetry, and what advantages does Hebrew poetry have over English poetry?**

Philosophical discourse, proverbs and sayings, praise and worship, even love poetry are presented in poetry. Hebrew poetry is easily translated into other languages because it is not dependent on rhyme, and it is better adapted than English poetry for different literary forms or purposes.

- **What is *parallelism*, and what are its basic forms in Hebrew poetry?**

Parallelism refers to the arrangement of ideas in Hebrew poetry to better convey impressions and meaning. It takes three forms: synonymous parallelism, antithetical parallelism, and synthetic parallelism.

Job—Story of Triumph over Harsh Troubles

Job was a good man who honestly tried to please God. Yet, in a single day, Job lost not only his wealth but also his children. Then he broke out in sores that covered his body. Job's friends were stunned. Their explanation: God must be punishing Job for some secret sin, for God is just, and God rewards the good and punishes the wicked. But Job was convinced that he didn't deserve what had happened, and his every belief about the nature of God was shaken. If tragedy and suffering can strike a man like Job, how can anyone believe that God is good?

The Challenge: Job 1-2

When God pointed Job out as a "blameless" man (Job 1:8 NKJV), a cynical Satan challenged God. Satan contended that being good paid off for Job. Strip away his wealth and his health, Satan argued, and Job would curse God to his face. God permitted Satan to attack Job. But rather than curse God, Job remained faithful. By the end of chapter 2, Satan had slunk off, defeated.

The Puzzle: Job 3-31

Job passed the test, but his suffering continued. When three old friends visited, the four of them explored the problem. The friends reasoned that since God is just, Job must be at fault. Job asserted his innocence and was driven by the friends' accusations to question God's fairness. At times, the wicked do prosper and the godly do suffer. But Job, too, believed God is just, which made his situation terrifying.

> If only my anguish could be weighed . . . ! It would surely outweigh the sand of the seas.
>
> Job 6:2–3 NIV
>
> After GOD had finished addressing Job, he turned to Eliphaz the Temanite and said, "I've had it with you and your two friends. I'm fed up! You haven't been honest either with me or about me—not the way my friend Job has."
>
> Job 42:7 MSG

One Way Out: Job 32–37

A young man named Elihu finally reacted. He argued that Job was wrong to question God's justice, but that the friends were wrong to assume Job's suffering had to be punishment for sin. After all, God could use pain to instruct and move people back onto the right path. Who knew what other benefits God might use suffering to achieve?

God's Response: Job 38–42

Finally, God confronted Job. God is so great, and man is so puny. How dare Job question God? Job surrendered, taking his place as a creature before his Creator. Job's friends were rebuked, Job was commended, and all Job had lost was restored twofold.

Something to Ponder

Why would God be angry with Job's three friends but not with Job? Possibly because the three were so intent on "protecting" God's reputation for fairness, they refused to consider the possibility that Job was innocent. It is okay to question beliefs about God within the context of faith. God is not threatened by our questions. Neither should we be.

Digging Deeper

From linguistic and other evidence, many people believe Job is the oldest Old Testament book. For instance, there is no mention of Moses or the Law in Job. Yet Job has a clear set of moral beliefs (Job 31). While details may differ from culture to culture, it is clear that human beings have a moral sense given by God and expressed in conscience (Romans 2:14-15).

Psalms—Songs of Passion, Joy, and Awe

Psalms is a collection of 150 poems, many of which were set to music and used in worship. The Hebrews called Psalms the *sepher tihillim*, the "book of praises." That name provides a clue to one value of the psalms today. In this day when we are so easily distracted by the demands and delights of modern life, the psalms focus our thoughts on God and lift our hearts to praise him. There is no more powerful book in the Bible for guiding us into a deeper and more personal relationship with him.

The Nature of the Psalms

The psalms are forged from personal experiences of God's Old Testament people. The psalms overflow with emotions, ranging from doubt and fear to comfort and joy. Many of the seventy-three psalms attributed to King David (about 1000 BC) provide a specific historical setting, as when he fled from his son Absalom (Psalm 3), or after he committed adultery with Bathsheba (Psalm 51). The psalms are utterly, totally true to life.

> I'm still in your presence, but you've taken my hand. You wisely and tenderly lead me, and then you bless me. You're all I want in heaven! You're all I want on earth! When my skin sags and my bones get brittle, God is rock-firm and faithful.
>
> Psalm 73:23–26 MSG

Values of the Psalms

The psalms teach us to be open and honest with God. The powerful emotional content of the psalms, including what many consider negative emotions like anger and jealousy, conveys an important lesson. We can be honest in our relationship with God, expressing exactly what we feel, being sure that he understands and cares. Rather than judging us, the God of the book of Psalms meets with us, and in his presence we sense a healing and transforming touch. In that presence we find perspective that enables us to master our emotions rather than be mastered by them.

The psalms focus our thoughts on God. The psalmists use powerful images to shape our awareness of how God relates to us. For the fearful, he is a fortress or a mighty rock in whose shadow we are sheltered. The Lord is our Shepherd, who cares for us throughout our lives. When we are discouraged, he is the one who lifts up our heads. When we are in danger, he is our shield. Whatever our situation or emotional state, the vision of God that shines so brightly through the psalms warms and comforts us.

The psalms teach us how to talk with God. There is no better way to enrich our worship than to pray along with the psalmist. Praying the psalms lifts our hearts to God, giving us confidence as we approach him, heightening our awareness of his presence.

Classifying Psalms

Some people classify psalms by their liturgical use: hymns for public worship (8, 67, for example), songs for private use to express thanksgiving (30; 34; 66) or lament (6; 13), and so on.

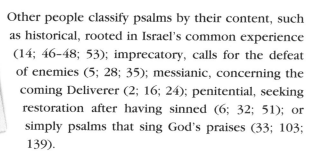

Other people classify psalms by their content, such as historical, rooted in Israel's common experience (14; 46–48; 53); imprecatory, calls for the defeat of enemies (5; 28; 35); messianic, concerning the coming Deliverer (2; 16; 24); penitential, seeking restoration after having sinned (6; 32; 51); or simply psalms that sing God's praises (33; 103; 139).

One of the most helpful ways of classifying psalms is by topic. Topical psalms deal with life issues, such as anger, disappointment, joy, and loneliness. Consult the Reader's Guide to the Psalms on page 120 to locate psalms that may be especially relevant to you.

Theological Contributions

The theology of the psalms is relational, and the psalms draw attention to who God is for us. God's essential character is celebrated repeatedly. God, the Creator of the universe (33:6-9; 95:3-7), is faithful (18:25, 28; 89:5-8), loving (36:5-7; 63:1-8), merciful (28:6-7; 86:15-17), and righteous (11:7; 145:17-21), always acting on behalf of his covenant people (77:11-15; 111:2-4, 6-9). He is a God his own can always count on.

> Let us sing psalms of praise to him. For the LORD is a great God, a great King above all gods.
>
> Psalm 95:2–3 NLT

The psalms uniquely meet us where we are in life. They reflect all the emotions we feel, they reshape our understanding, and they guide us to make wise choices. These magnificent poems gently lead us to God, who can transform us and our circumstances.

Myth Buster

Some challenge the reliability of the Bible on the basis of various images in the Psalms. References like "the rising of the sun" (Psalm 50:1 NIV) are claimed to demonstrate scientific errors in Scripture, while frequent references to safety found "in the shadow of your [God's] wings" (Psalm 36:7 NIV) are taken as literal descriptions that conflict with other pictures of Israel's God. Such challenges have been answered easily. References to the sun's rising are phenomenological, that is, they describe what we see, not what actually happens. And anyone who reads poetry understands that poetic language uses similes and other figures of speech to convey that which is not intended to be taken literally.

Digging Deeper

- The psalms are poetry.

- All but thirty-four psalms have descriptive superscriptions.

- Untranslated words in superscriptions, like *Maskil*, probably refer to musical genre or arrangements.

- *Selah* in some psalms may mean "pause, and think about it."

- The five books of psalms indicated by Roman numerals mark groups added to the collection at different times.

- Martin Luther saw psalms as a revelation of the hearts of all saints.

- Archaeological finds of poetic literature in parallel cultures suggest psalms could be among the earliest biblical literature.

Reader's Guide to the Psalms

When You Are . . .	Read Psalms . . .
Angry	4; 17; 28; 36; 109
Anxious	2; 11; 27; 46; 49; 121
Disappointed	16; 92; 102; 130
Discouraged	12; 45; 55; 86; 107
Grieving	6; 31; 71; 77; 94
Impatient	4; 5; 37; 89; 123
Insecure	34; 84; 91
Joyful	33; 47; 84; 97; 98; 148
Lonely	3; 13; 17; 25; 69; 91
Mistreated	7; 9; 17; 35; 56; 94
Seeking God	8; 19; 29; 65; 89; 103
Sick	22; 23; 41; 116
Stressed	12; 24; 31; 43; 56; 84
Thankful	30; 33; 40; 66; 96; 113
Troubled	10; 86; 90; 94; 126
Uncertain	1; 25; 26; 37; 101; 119
Weak	4; 23; 62; 70; 102; 138

Proverbs—Pithy Principles of Right and Wrong

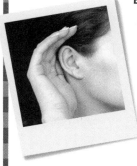

Every culture seems to develop pithy sayings packed with practical advice. Ben Franklin is credited with many of these sayings, sayings such as "A stitch in time saves nine" and "Well begun is half done." The ancient Hebrews were partial to packaging advice in poetic couplets like those we find in the book of Proverbs. These sayings express general principles for getting along in this world that are true whether or not one is a believer. Wise men and women still heed these insights that were recorded some three thousand years ago.

Author and Theme

Tradition and the text ascribe most of these sayings to King Solomon, who earned a reputation as the world's wisest man (2 Chronicles 9:22). The stated purpose of Proverbs is to help the reader "get wisdom," that wisdom might "save you from the ways of wicked men" (Proverbs 2:12 NIV). The wisdom Proverbs is concerned with is practical, the good common sense that will help a person make choices that benefit rather than harm him.

> [Wisdom] is more precious than rubies, and all the things you may desire cannot compare with her. Length of days is in her right hand, in her left hand riches and honor.
>
> Proverbs 3:15–16 NKJV
>
> My child, listen closely to my teachings and learn common sense. My advice is useful, so don't turn away.
>
> Proverbs 4:1–2 CEV

Themes of the Proverbs

Various proverbs comment on everything from parent-child relationships to laziness, relationships with neighbors to poverty. Sayings typically are scattered through the book rather than assembled by topics, although early chapters do contain extended thoughts on the value of wisdom (1–4; 8–9) and warnings against sexual promiscuity (5; 6:20–7:27).

While it's possible to simply read through a chapter of Proverbs and sample its many topics, it is fascinating to collect proverbs on a single theme.

Warning!

When reading Proverbs there are several things to keep in mind: (1) Proverbs are not promises. They are general principles. (2) As general principles, they do have exceptions. While it is usually true that "a soft answer turns away wrath" (Proverbs 15:1 NKJV), that's not always the case. (3) Proverbs express universal principles. Anyone who follows their advice, believer or not, will lead a happier and less stressful life. (4) "The fear of the LORD is the beginning of knowledge" (Proverbs 1:7 NKJV). A person who respects God is far more likely to live by the principles the book of Proverbs distills.

Final Thoughts

Everyone learns from experience. But it is far less painful to learn from the experiences of others than from our own. Reading and thinking about the sayings in the book of Proverbs sum up what others have learned from experience.

Themes in Proverbs

Theme	Chapter and Verse
Discipline	3:11–12; 5:12–14; 6:23; 9:7–10; 10:17; 12:1; 13:18; 24; 15:5, 10, 32; 19:18; 22:15; 23:13–14; 27:5; 29:15
Friendship	1:10–19; 12:26; 13:20; 16:28; 17:17; 18:1, 24; 19:7; 22:11; 27:6; 10
Work	12:11, 14, 24, 27; 14:23; 16:26; 18:9; 22:29; 27:18; 23–27

Ecclesiastes—Writings of Discernment and Knowledge

Many find the little book of Ecclesiastes puzzling. Yet Solomon defined exactly what he intended to do. He would study and "explore by wisdom all that is done under heaven" (Ecclesiastes 1:13 NIV). This book is the result of an intense search conducted by history's wisest man using all his great intellectual gifts. But the search was limited to data he gained by observation and personal experiences "under heaven." Solomon purposely ruled out divine revelation, whose origin is heaven. And what Solomon hoped to find was meaning for a human life lived apart from God!

Meaningless! Meaningless!

Solomon was shaken by his discovery that apart from God human life has no meaning. Solomon tasted every pleasure, measured his achievements, and found it all empty (chapters 1–2). He looked ahead and realized he would be forgotten; nothing he had done affected the rhythm of life as established by God (chapter 3). Neither power, nor wealth, nor wisdom can satisfy.

Discouraged, Solomon admitted that some courses in life are better than others (chapters 8–11). But while these may smooth our path here, every person is vulnerable to injustice, and nothing can provide the meaning our hearts yearn for.

In the few days of our meaningless lives, who knows how our days can best be spent? Our lives are like a shadow. Who can tell what will happen on this earth after we are gone?

Ecclesiastes 6:12 NLT

We each go to our eternal home.

Ecclesiastes 12:5 CEV

What, then, can a person do? Solomon said to appreciate the Creator's gifts during youth, for old age, decrepitude, and death lie ahead. As for meaning, human life has none. All is meaningless.

This Is in the Bible?

When we compare Ecclesiastes with other Scripture, we are jarred by the contrasting viewpoints. Solomon even seems to question life after death, asking, "Who really knows if our spirits go up and the spirits of animals go down into the earth?" (Ecclesiastes 3:21 CEV). Yet inspiration of Scripture guarantees an accurate account of Solomon's thinking. What Ecclesiastes contributes to the canon of Scripture is a confirmation of its consistent testimony. Human beings find meaning in life through a personal relationship with God. Apart from him, as Solomon discovered, life truly is meaningless.

Final Thoughts

Ecclesiastes may well be a good book to suggest to an unhappy friend. Why? Because often discovering a need for God is a first step toward finding hope and fulfillment in him. Nothing compares to the power of this little book to bring home the emptiness of life apart from God.

Something to Ponder

Solomon began his rule totally dedicated to God. How could he possibly pen such a pessimistic book? Solomon married many foreign wives (1 Kings 11). It was good politics to seal treaties with weddings, but it was folly. In time Solomon's wives led him into idolatry, and Solomon lost contact with God. Solomon applied his great intel-  lect to seek meaning apart from God. At the end of his life a despairing Solomon correctly concluded that life apart from God is essentially meaningless.

Song of Solomon—Collection of Love Poems

Love shapes the lyrics of our popular music and fills book after book of poetry. Still, somehow we don't expect to discover love poetry in Scripture. That may be one reason this collection of love songs has been treated by Jews and Christians alike as allegory, symbolic of God's love for Israel or Jesus' love for the church. On its surface, though, Song of Solomon, also called Song of Songs, captures the yearning of two young lovers who share the emotional highs and lows known by lovers everywhere.

The Tale

The Song of Solomon has a story to tell. It pictures a young ruler wandering incognito who meets a beautiful country girl. The two fall passionately in love, and the early stanzas are filled with each one's praises for the other. Then the young ruler leaves, and his bride-to-be is desolate. Has he abandoned her? No! For suddenly he reappears, not as a commoner but in his glory as king. He lifts her up beside him as his bride, to live together in unbroken communion.

My dove, my virtuous one, is unique.

Song of Songs 6:9 HCSB

Have respect for marriage. Always be faithful to your partner.

Hebrews 13:4 CEV

As Allegory

It's easy to see why the poem has been taken as allegory. In the Old Testament, Israel is portrayed as the wife of the Lord, destined to be united with him at history's end (Isaiah 54:5–6). And the New Testament calls the church the bride of Christ, who will claim her at his return (Revelation 18:23). These biblical images fit too perfectly with the Song of Solomon to be ignored.

As Personal Experience

At the same time, the passion and delight two people find in each other is too familiar to imagine that the Song of Solomon didn't grow out of the writers' personal experience. We sense a familiar fervor, an ardor that is too authentic to be anything less than genuine. In the Song of Solomon we also sense a validation of human love, a divine stamp of approval on the intimacy intended by God when he created human beings male and female.

Final Thoughts

One of the values of the Song of Solomon is to help us recapture the romance of falling in love. This is sorely needed in our society. When any culture divorces sex from love and marriage, one of God's greatest gifts is perverted, and lasting joy is traded for temporary titillation.

Something to Ponder

It is ironic that this book is ascribed to Solomon, for at the end of his life that king was led astray by his passion for his many foreign brides (1 Kings 11). How different his story and that of his kingdom might have been had Solomon followed his own advice, to "take pleasure in the wife of your youth," to "let her breasts always satisfy you," and to be "lost in her love forever" (Proverbs 5:18–19 HCSB).

The Prophets

God raised up men and women throughout Israel's history. He spoke through them to his people with powerful words of guidance, rebuke, and encouragement.

Contents

Timely Messages from God 129

Isaiah—Words of Hope 131

Jeremiah and Lamentations—Light in Darkness................. 135

Ezekiel—Darkness and Dawn.. 139

Daniel—Visions of History to Come 141

Minor Prophets in Israel—Jonah, Amos, and Hosea 143

Minor Prophets in Judah—Obadiah, Joel, Micah,
Nahum, Habakkuk, and Zephaniah..................................... 147

Prophets After the Exile—Haggai, Zechariah,
and Malachi 151

Know this first of all, that no prophecy of Scripture
is a matter of one's own interpretation, for no prophecy
was ever made by an act of human will, but men
moved by the Holy Spirit spoke from God.

2 Peter 1:20–21 NASB

Timely Messages from God

The Ten Commandments (Exodus 20) guided the choices of Old Testament believers. But these couldn't cover every situation that arose. Sometimes God's people faced situations in which they simply didn't know what to do. So God made provision for timely special messages to his Old Testament people. The high priest's vest contained a pocket holding Urim and Thummim, objects that provided yes or no answers to questions asked of God (Exodus 28:30; Numbers 27:21). But most special messages came through spokespersons called *prophets*. The prophet's mission was to convey timely guidance, warning, or encouragement that applied directly to the present situation.

Prophecy and Prediction

Prediction is an important element in prophecy. Prediction of events to take place in the near future helped distinguish true from false prophets.

Deuteronomy 18:17-21 provides three tests: A true prophet (1) must be a Jew, (2) must speak in the name of the Lord, and (3) what he or she predicts must come to pass. Near-at-hand predictions authenticated a prophet's claim to be God's spokesperson. A good example is found in Jeremiah 28.

> I will give my message to that prophet, who will tell the people exactly what I have said.
>
> Deuteronomy 18:18 CEV
>
> The LORD, the God of their ancestors, repeatedly sent his prophets to warn them.
>
> 2 Chronicles 36:15 NLT

Generally, predictions of distant events provided encouragement or stimulated holy living in view of what God intended to accomplish. For us, fulfilled prophecy is a source of confidence in the supernatural origin of Scripture.

The Need for Special Guidance

There are times when we are uncertain about choices that will impact our future. At such times, we yearn for supernatural guidance. In the world of the Bible, most societies looked to occult practices for guidance. But Deuteronomy 18 called all occult activities detestable and forbade relying on them. In their place, God promised to send prophets to guide his people. God kept his word. But too often the Israelites refused to heed the prophets.

Myth Buster

Many people assume that the essential purpose of prophecy is to describe future events. Yet foretelling the future was only one aspect of the ministry of the biblical prophets. The prophets explained the reasons for national disasters, urged repentance and faithfulness to God, and conveyed his promises to people of his own time. Revelations of the future underlined the contemporary message. Understanding something of the fixed elements of God's plan for "tomorrow" was almost always intended to motivate people's response to God in the "now."

Check Your Understanding

- **What is the role of a prophet, and what are the three tests he or she must pass?**

Prophets are to provide special guidance in specific situations. The three tests for a true prophet are (1) a true prophet must be a Jew, (2) a true prophet must speak in the name of God, and (3) what the prophet says must come true.

- **What two kinds of predictive prophecy are there, and what are the functions of the two predictive prophecies?**

Predictions fall into two categories: (1) near-at-hand predictions and (2) distant-future predictions. Near-at-hand predictions authenticate the prophet as a spokesperson of God. Distant-future predictions encourage, warn, or guide present decisions.

Isaiah—Words of Hope

The book of Isaiah begins with a dreaded drum roll. God's people were hauled into court, indicted, and charged as "a people loaded with guilt, a brood of evildoers" (1:4 NIV). A sense of impending doom hangs over the first half of the book, though broken now and then by a ray of sunshine. But then the clouds of judgment clear, and the second half of Isaiah glows with promise. Despite Israel's failure, God intends to bless his chosen people and through them the entire world.

⚹

The Man and His Times

Isaiah was called to be a prophet the year King Uzziah died (739 BC). Isaiah ministered to several kings and preached against foreign alliances (7:1–18). Tradition says he was martyred by King Manasseh about 480 BC.

During the early years of Isaiah's ministry, both Israel and Judah prospered. But Isaiah sensed approaching doom and devoted his ministry to calling both Hebrew kingdoms to repentance. Sermons from this period are recorded in Isaiah 1–35.

I have spoken; so I will also bring it about. I have planned it; I will also do it.

Isaiah 46:11 HCSB

The LORD longs to be gracious to you; he rises to show you compassion. . . . Blessed are all who wait for him!

Isaiah 30:18 NIV

Isaiah's warnings were ignored in the north, but under godly King Hezekiah, Judah experienced a spiritual revival. The revival came just in time. Mighty Assyria was pushing southward, Israel fell to the invaders, and the Assyrians pressed on into Judah. The fortress cities protecting Judah's border fell, and the tidal wave seemed about to engulf Jerusalem when God intervened (Isaiah 36–39). The tiny southern Hebrew kingdom survived.

Hezekiah was succeeded by his son Manasseh. It was during Manasseh's reign that Isaiah penned chapters 40–66 of his book. These chapters' theme, style, vocabulary, and outlook are so different from the early chapters that scholars have questioned Isaiah's authorship, something neither Jews nor Christians questioned until the eighteenth century.

Unifying Themes in Isaiah

Differences of style and vocabulary cannot disguise the unifying themes woven through the entire book of Isaiah. Both major sections of Isaiah focus our attention on a future Savior King. Born of a virgin (7:14), bearing titles of deity (9:6), he will establish justice (11:1–16). As Servant of the Lord, he will complete Israel's failed mission (42; 49). Rejected by Israel, the coming Deliverer will pour out his life to bear the sins of many and restore humankind's lost relationship with God (53).

Understanding Isaiah

In chapters 1–35 the enemy is Assyria, and the danger is imminent. In chapters 40–66, the enemy is Babylon, and the danger lies some hundred years in the future. This shift in perspective, along with critics' doubts about the possibility of prophetic vision, has contributed to the notion that Isaiah was written by at least two and possibly more authors. However, the book is quoted some fifty times by New Testament writers as the work of Isaiah.

Isaiah's writing is beautiful, powerful, and extremely moving. Isaiah, like many Old Testament prophetic books, is largely poetry interspersed with prose segments. Yet it is impossible to read the exalted language of this great prophet without being drawn into the emotions that Isaiah and God shared, emotions that ran the gamut from pain and anger to intense love and hope. Isaiah never forgot that undergirding God's relationship with his people was a commitment that could never falter.

Theological Contributions

A theme that runs throughout the book is God's sovereignty. God alone can reveal "the end from the beginning," for he controls history and promises, "My purpose will stand" (46:10 NIV). As we read Isaiah, we realize that this is one of the most comforting truths in the Bible. For God's purpose is to bless, something we realize as we read Isaiah's words of hope, offering

> Sing to the LORD a new song, sing His praise from the end of the earth!
>
> Isaiah 42:10 NASB

comfort for today and confidence in tomorrow. When the all-powerful God is ours and we are his, the knowledge that he is in control stimulates our praise.

Hope in Scripture isn't wishful thinking. Rather, the biblical term is one of expectation. In times of uncertainty and distress, hope is a reminder that God is faithful and a reassurance that we can trust him.

Words of Hope in Isaiah

Words of Hope	Isaiah
God's invitation to Israel	1:2–20
God's promise of peace	9:1–7
God's plans for the Messiah	11:1–9
God's gift of strength	40:18–31
God's certain blessing	46:5–13
Jesus' sacrifice foretold	53:4–12
God's new creation	65:17–25

Digging Deeper

God's sovereignty is illustrated in fulfilled prophecy. Centuries before Jesus, Isaiah foretold his virgin birth (Isaiah 7:14) in Bethlehem (Micah 5:2). He was to be descended from David (Isaiah 9:6-7), rejected by his own people (Isaiah 6:10; 53:1-3), and betrayed by a friend (Zechariah 11:12-13). He would be put to death with criminals (Isaiah 53:9, 12) but buried with the rich (Isaiah 53:9). These and dozens of other details about Jesus' birth, life, and death found in the Old Testament took place as predicted. God keeps his promises always. Our future is secure.

Something to Ponder

To Old Testament people, names indicated something about the essence of the person or thing named. Isaiah used a number of names for God, and each helps us better understand the passage where the name is used. Thus where Isaiah identified the Lord as the "Holy one of Israel," he alerted us to the fact that the passage expresses something important about God's holiness. Names of God found in Isaiah include "Lord Almighty," "God of Jacob," "Sovereign Lord," "everlasting God," "Redeemer," "Savior," and many others. Understanding the significance of names helps us gain the most from Bible reading.

Jeremiah and Lamentations—Light in Darkness

There are times when the present seems so dark that we are driven to despair. It was like this for the prophet Jeremiah, who ministered during the last forty years of Judah's existence. His warnings ignored, his patriotism challenged, the man who has been called "the Weeping Prophet" was scorned and imprisoned. Through it all, Jeremiah was sustained by faith, and he was given the privilege of revealing a unique and glorious promise, a promise that we claim today in Jesus.

The Man and His Time

Judah was a tiny state on the southern border of the great but weakening Assyrian Empire. When Assyrian forces were crushed at the battle of Carchemish in 605 BC, an expansionist Babylonian Empire replaced the Assyrian Empire, and Judah suffered a series of invasions that culminated in the total destruction of Jerusalem in 587 BC. The earlier revival led by King Josiah (640–609 BC) flickered and died upon that king's death, and Jeremiah witnessed the moral and spiritual collapse of his nation. In 627 BC, Jeremiah was called to be a prophet (Jeremiah 1:1–16), to announce that God intended to use Babylon to punish his straying people. But when Jeremiah urged submission to the Babylonians, he was reviled, threatened, and imprisoned.

The LORD said: I have made my decision, and I won't change my mind.

Jeremiah 4:27 CEV

I have loved you with an everlasting love; therefore with lovingkindness I have drawn you. Again I will build you, and you shall be rebuilt.

Jeremiah 31:3–4 NKJV

Jeremiah's lonely stand against popular opinion exerted intense pressure on the prophet. He often shared his feelings of desolation with God and with others. Yet Jeremiah remained faithful to his mission, and he balanced passages telling of personal anguish with confessions of stead-fast faith in God. Only Jeremiah's awareness of who God is enabled him to go on.

In the end, Jeremiah was vindicated. The Babylonians swept into Judah, destroyed the city and the temple, and deported the remaining population.

Light in Darkness

Little Judah was about to be crushed by brutal enemy forces and its population killed or deported to Babylon. Soon the people who had ignored Jeremiah's warnings were themselves caught up in despair. But God spoke through Jeremiah to make a promise that would serve future generations as a beacon of hope.

Centuries earlier God had given Abraham covenant promises, formal commitments assuring Abraham that God would bless his descendants and  through them the whole world. God expanded on these promises in the Davidic covenant (2 Samuel 7), revealing that the agent of blessing would be a King, a Messiah to be born from David's line. Through Jeremiah, in what is called the new covenant, God revealed that the core of the promised blessing was to be forgive-ness and transformation. When the new covenant was enacted, Jeremiah promised, no longer would God's standards of right and wrong be expressed simply in an external code. Instead, God would forgive sins and through an inner transformation make people truly good.

The New Testament book of Hebrews explains that this promised covenant was enacted at the Cross, and that inner transformation is avail-able today through faith in Jesus.

The New Covenant

Here is *The Message* paraphrase of God's decree: "This is the brand-new covenant that I will make with Israel when the time comes. I will put my law within them—write it on their hearts!—and be their God.

And they will be my people. They will no longer go around setting up schools to teach each other about GOD. They'll know me firsthand, the dull and the bright, the smart and the slow. I'll wipe the slate clean for each of them. I'll forget they ever sinned!" (Jeremiah 31:33-34 MSG).

Reading Jeremiah

Jeremiah is a lengthy book, but its central themes are summed up in key chapters. To meet this man whose faith enabled him to survive emotional turmoil, read Jeremiah 10:23-24; 11:18-12:6; 15:10-21; 17:9-18; 18:18-23; and 20:7-18.

Sing to the LORD! Praise the LORD, for He rescues the life of the needy from the hand of evil people.

Jeremiah 20:13 HCSB

To understand the spiritual and moral conditions that cried out for divine judgment, read Jeremiah 2:1-3:5, along with chapters 23 and 33. Even after Judah fell, the people refused to listen to God's prophet (Jeremiah 37-44). But for a picture of the Jews' bright future foreseen by Jeremiah, read Jeremiah 30-33.

Lamentations

Despite encouragement given in Jeremiah's vision of the future, the men and women who were exiled to Babylon grieved for their lost homeland. Their regret was captured in the five dirge (funereal) poems that make up the little book of Lamentations. Tradition says that after Jerusalem's fall, Jeremiah made his way to Babylon, where he penned these poems.

Final Thoughts

None of us are immune to discouragement or the pain of rejection by loved ones. All of us at times can identify with Jeremiah, the Weeping Prophet. But Jeremiah's story reminds us that each of us can be sustained by trust in God, even as Jeremiah's words focus on a future filled with hope.

Digging Deeper

Dr. Michael Jursa was studying some cuneiform tablets in the Babylonian collection of the British Museum when he found a reference to a "chief eunuch." It was the same person identified in Jeremiah 39:3 as one of the high officials who were with the king of Babylon when Jerusalem fell in 587 BC. Biblical archaeologists consider the tablets primary sources that confirm the Bible's accuracy regarding an important historical person.

Jeremiah 1:15 predicts that "kings will come and set up their thrones in the entrance of the gates of Jerusalem" (NIV). Forty years later the prediction came true (Jeremiah 39), a fact confirmed by the discovery of the name of the high Babylonian official who was present on a cuneiform tablet by Dr. Michael Jursa.

Something to Ponder

Jeremiah seems to be a contradiction, a man of tears and yet of hope. His entire ministry was predicated on his conviction that Jerusalem and Judah were doomed and that the present generation would suffer terribly at the hands of Babylonian armies. Yet he recorded one of the most encouraging promises found in Scripture: "'I know  the plans I have for you,' declares the LORD, 'plans to prosper you and not to harm you, plans to give you hope and a future'" (Jeremiah 29:11 NIV). Today may be dark. But tomorrow holds a brighter dawn.

Ezekiel—Darkness and Dawn

Ezekiel's family was among the many leading families taken captive to Babylon in 597 BC. Back in Judah, a puppet king was placed on the throne. The captives remained optimistic about the possibility of a return home. Like those in the homeland, they reasoned that because God's temple was in Jerusalem, God would defend the city, come what may. When Ezekiel began predicting the fall of the city and the destruction of the temple, his message was rejected by the elders of his people.

✳

The Man and His Message

In Judah, Jeremiah urged submission to Babylon. Among the captives in Babylon, thirty-year-old Ezekiel preached the same message. The Jews must put down roots in Babylon, for Judah would fall and its population would join the captives. In 586 BC, Jerusalem did fall, and for thirteen years Ezekiel was silent. Then Ezekiel spoke out again, this time to describe a future in which the Jews would be regathered to their homeland and a glorious new temple erected. These themes create a natural division in the book of Ezekiel, with chapters 1–32 emphasizing approaching doom, and chapters 33–36 a coming dawn.

Preach my message to them, whether they choose to listen or not.

Ezekiel 2:7 CEV

I will make a covenant of peace with them, an everlasting covenant. . . . I will put my Temple among them forever.

Ezekiel 37:26 NLT

God in Ezekiel

The captives were convinced that Jerusalem would not fall, for it held God's temple, the visible symbol of his presence on earth. But in a powerful vision recorded in chapters 8–11, Ezekiel saw idolatry that desecrated the temple, and watched as the glory of the Lord rose over the city and then departed, leaving the temple an empty shell. The God of Israel is not limited to a single place, nor does he dwell among a people who refuse to honor him.

This vision and other striking visions of God himself (Ezekiel 1; 8) in the first half of the book emphasize a holiness of God that his people would relearn through the coming judgment. Yet, in the second half of Ezekiel, we see a God who remains faithful, who will restore his people to their land, and who will again welcome their worship.

Final Thoughts

The phrase "you will know that I am the Lord" appears some fifty times in Ezekiel. The people of Ezekiel's time had a distorted knowledge of a God they had reshaped to fit their own imaginations. Sometimes, it takes a seeming disaster to turn a people back to God, to rediscover who he really is.

Something to Ponder

Do parents fix the destiny of a child? Ezekiel 18 reminds us that we have the power to choose whether to follow the example of our parents, be that example good or bad. Even as war and famine ravaged Jerusalem, God promised to preserve the life of the individual who did what was just and right. God doesn't judge you by your parents. God evaluates "each of you according to his own ways" (Ezekiel 33:20 NIV).

Daniel—Visions of History to Come

As a promising teenager, Daniel was taken to Babylon and enrolled in the king's academy to be trained for government service. God gave him prophetic gifts, and when Daniel described a dream of Nebuchadnezzar's and revealed its meaning, he was quickly promoted. Throughout his long life, the influential Daniel served in the governments of dominant world empires. But Daniel's greatest contribution was to biblical prophecy. In stunning detail, he described the kingdoms that would dominate the East until the appearance of the promised Messiah.

The Man and His Mission

In 605 BC, Daniel was among the first Jews deported to Babylon. Stories of his faithfulness to God and of the events that lifted him to prominence are told in the first six chapters of his book. These are the stories every Sunday school student knows. Chapters 7–8 relate a series of visions Daniel had concerning future empires that would control the Holy Land until the Messiah appeared. The descriptions are so detailed and accurate that some critics insist the book must have been written after the events described took place. Yet archaeological discoveries have shown that the writer had an intimate acquaintance within the courts of Babylon and Persia, providing details that no writer centuries removed would have been familiar with. For those who believe in a God who can reveal the future, Daniel's predictions confirm Scripture's reliability rather than call it into question.

> There is a God in heaven who reveals mysteries.
>
> Daniel 2:28 NASB
>
> Go your way till the end; for you shall rest, and will arise to your inheritance of the end of the days.
>
> Daniel 12:13 NKJV

One of the most stunning of his prophecies is found in Daniel 9:20–27. This prophecy specifies that seventy sevens of years (490 years) are to pass from a future decree to rebuild Jerusalem until the appearance, and then the "cutting off," of the Messiah. Sir Robert Anderson, in a book titled *The Coming Prince*, calculated the years and days, and he found that the predicted date corresponds to the baptism of Jesus (Matthew 4; Luke 4), whose life was "cut off" at the Cross. Prophecies in chapters 11 and 12 of Daniel concern history's end, and await a still-future fulfillment.

Final Thoughts

The book of Daniel speaks to us on several levels. Its stories of Daniel's life provide examples for us to follow, and its prophetic revelations encourage us, for they remind us that whatever happens, God has not lost control of world events.

Something to Ponder

Daniel reminds us of the good that can be accomplished through service in government. Daniel earned a reputation for honesty and integrity. Daniel was open about his faith. These traits won him the respect of the most powerful men in the ancient world and enabled him to share his faith with them. Every nation needs men and women with Daniel-like qualities in leadership roles.

Minor Prophets in Israel—Jonah, Amos, and Hosea

When the united Hebrew kingdom divided on the death of Solomon, the ruler of the northern kingdom, Israel, set a disastrous course. He instituted a religious system that counterfeited the one established in the Old Testament. Every king of Israel continued the corrupt practices that Jeroboam I established, and the nation experienced continuous moral and spiritual decline. Still, rather than abandon a people who had abandoned him, God sent prophets to Israel, calling his people to return. But the kings and people of the north were reluctant to hear.

"Minor" Prophets

The prophetic books of the Old Testament are divided between *Major* and *Minor* Prophets, based mainly on the length of each book. Isaiah, Jeremiah, Ezekiel, and Daniel are considered the Major Prophets. The writers of the other prophetic books—such as Jonah, Amos, and Hosea—are classified as the Minor Prophets.

I'd rather for you to be faithful and to know me than to offer sacrifices.

Hosea 6:6 CEV

Hate evil and love good, then work it out in the public square.

Amos 5:15 MSG

Many prophets mentioned in the Old Testament, like Elijah, who ministered in Israel during the reign of King Ahab (1 Kings 17–21), left no writings of their own. Such prophets are often called *speaking* prophets, and we find their stories in the Bible books that recount the history of the Hebrew kings (2 Samuel; 1 and 2 Kings; 1 and 2 Chronicles).

Both speaking and writing prophets ministered to the people of their own time, delivering vital messages from God to their contemporaries.

Jonah

Jonah prophesied in Israel during the prosperous reign of Jeroboam II and predicted military victories for Israel (2 Kings 14:25). Then Jonah was told to go north to Nineveh, the capital of Assyria, and announce that God intended to destroy that great city in thirty days. Instead, Jonah took a ship south. God intervened, and the reluctant prophet was swallowed by a great fish and thrown up on a northern shore. Finally,

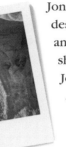

Jonah obeyed, but when he announced the city's destruction, the king and people of Nineveh repented and no judgment came. Angry with God at the grace shown the great enemy of his nation, the patriotic Jonah sulked.

Withholding judgment on Nineveh conveyed a powerful message to Israel. Would not the God who was gracious to his people's enemy be even more gracious to a repentant Israel? The invitation to Israel implicit in Nineveh's experience was ignored. God's people failed to repent, and in 722 BC judgment came in the form of an invading Assyrian army.

Amos

Amos was a rancher in Judah when God called him to prophesy in Israel. Amos condemned the counterfeit worship practices of the northern kingdom, but he focused attention on the injustice that marred that society. The poor were systematically oppressed, morals were corrupt, and the wealthy were indifferent to the suffering of their fellow Israelites. Such a society cried out for judgment, and judgment would surely come. Furious, Israel's religious and secular officials demanded that Amos leave the country.

Hosea

Hosea was told by God to marry a woman who was, or who would become, a prostitute. They had several children together, but then the wife, Gomer, abandoned her husband for a series of lovers. Through it all, Hosea continued to pursue his wife, even providing for her needs as she consorted with his rivals.

In emotionally powerful passages, God compared his experience with Israel to Hosea's experience with Gomer. Their beloveds had been unfaithful and had broken their husbands' hearts. But neither God nor Hosea would give up until the straying wives were returned home to stay.

Common Themes

These and most other Minor Prophets focus on the failings of God's people, warn of impending judgment, and yet invite repentance and return. The Minor Prophets also tend to end on a positive note. Even should a present generation refuse to repent and experience judgment, God would bless his people in the end. In the encouraging last words of Amos: "I'll make Israel prosper again. You will rebuild your

> When God saw that the people had stopped doing evil things, he had pity and did not destroy them as he had planned.
>
> Jonah 3:10 CEV

towns and live in them. You will drink wine from your own vineyards and eat the fruit you grow. I'll plant your roots deep in the land I have given you, and you won't ever be uprooted again" (Amos 9:14–15 CEV).

Final Thoughts

Believers are called to care about others as God cares about them. Amos's passionate demand that Israel correct injustice, Hosea's call to love sinners, and the lesson taught to Jonah that even the most wicked can repent and be accepted by a compassionate God all express attitudes Christians are to reflect today.

Digging Deeper

Many Christians can identify with Jonah as a patriot who loved his country. He predicted the military victories that King Jeroboam II had won, victories that reduced crushing pressures under which the people of Israel had lived. So when told to go to Nineveh, the capital of a powerful enemy state, Jonah put his country first. Many centuries later, Saint Augustine, the great Christian theologian, warned against confusing the City of God with the City of Man as pagan enemies battered the Christianized Roman Empire. Nations rise and fall, but God continues to build his kingdom. Love of country is good, but we should never view our nation as essential to the spiritual kingdom God is forming in history.

Insights into God and Society

Hosea's insight into God's heart:
"Start all over: Love your wife again, your wife who's in bed with her latest boyfriend, your cheating wife. Love her the way I, GOD, love the Israelite people, even as they flirt and party with every god that takes their fancy" (Hosea 3:1 MSG).

Amos's insight into Israelite society:
"How you hate honest judges! How you despise people who tell the truth! You trample the poor, stealing their grain through taxes and unfair rent. Therefore, though you build beautiful stone houses, you will never live in them. Though you plant lush vineyards, you will never drink wine from them. For I know the vast number of your sins and the depth of your rebellions. You oppress good people by taking bribes and deprive the poor of justice in the courts" (Amos 5:10–12 NLT).

Minor Prophets in Judah—
Obadiah, Joel, Micah, Nahum, Habakkuk, and Zephaniah

On Solomon's death only two Israelite tribes remained committed to his son, Rehoboam. Yet for nearly four hundred years a descendant of David ruled Judah, the southern Hebrew kingdom. Many of Judah's kings were indifferent to biblical religion. At critical times, however, godly kings emerged to lead revivals that preserved the nation. Some of these revivals are associated with the ministry of those we call minor prophets.

Obadiah

The Edomites were cousins to the Jews, descendants of Esau, the brother of Abraham's son Isaac. Yet from the time of Moses, the Edomites displayed a persistent hostility toward the Israel-ites. The book of Obadiah predicts God's judgment of Edom for cheer-ing on and then taking part in the capture of Jerusalem by foreign enemies. Two possible attacks on Jerusalem fit the book's descrip-tion, so it is difficult to date Obadiah with any certainty. Whatever the date, the prophet had a firm basis for his prediction. The Abrahamic covenant committed God to bless those who blessed Israel, and to curse those who cursed them (Genesis 12:3).

Why are You silent while one who is wicked swallows up one who is more righteous than himself?

Habakkuk 1:13 HCSB

Do not gloat over me, my enemies! . . . Though I sit in darkness, the LORD will be my light.

Micah 7:8 NLT

Joel

A cloud of locusts settled on Judah, devouring every blade of grass and leaving the land desolate (chapter 1). The locusts stimulated a vision of an invading army that would devastate the Holy Land at history's end (chapter 2). The date Joel wrote is unknown, but other prophets confirmed his vision of dark days ahead.

Micah

Micah was a contemporary of Isaiah. Both experienced Judah's revival under King Hezekiah. Micah also reflects themes of the northern prophets Amos ("do justice") and Hosea ("return to me"). Micah, like Joel, saw disaster ahead. But also like Joel, he foresaw a glorious future emerge from the darkness (Micah 7:8-13; Joel 3:9-21).

Nahum

Nahum wrote in the 650s BC. His three brief chapters describe the fall of Nineveh, capital of Assyria. Some hundred years earlier, Isaiah also had spoken of God's judgment of Assyria for that nation's brutality toward Israel (Isaiah 10:5-19; 30:27-33; 31:5-9; 37:21-35).

Habakkuk

Judah had experienced a religious revival under King Josiah. But Habakkuk remained troubled. The revival failed to change Judah's society, and Habakkuk wondered how long God could permit his people to do evil. God revealed that at that moment he was raising up Babylon, a nation that would attack Judah. Habakkuk was satisfied; the invasion would discipline and purify God's people. But then the prophet had a disturbing thought. The Babylonians were even more wicked than the Jews! What did God intend to do about them?

Chapter 1 contains God's answer to Habakkuk. Even as the Babylonians triumphed, God was judging them. Each success inflamed their desire; they could never find satisfaction. And their treatment of others turned everyone against them, so their turn would come. Again Habakkuk was satisfied with God's explanation.

But then God gave the prophet visions of past judgments, and Habakkuk trembled. He finally realized how terrible the coming judgment was to be for himself as well as his nation. In that day, only trust in God would enable him to survive (chapter 3).

Zephaniah

Like Habakkuk, Zephaniah prophesied during the reign of godly King Hezekiah. He was convinced that Judah was doomed to suffer divine judgment. So Zephaniah appealed to individuals who might respond to God's promise of mercy and to those who would survive the coming time of judgment. The days immediately ahead would be dark indeed (Zephaniah 3:1-7). But just beyond would be God's eternal kingdom (Zephaniah 3:8-20).

The Minor Prophets' Moral Vision

The minor prophets ministered at different times and in different circumstances. Yet they shared a common moral vision. Each was convinced that God had established standards of right and wrong that humans were responsible to live by. Each was convinced that God held human beings responsible, and that he was bound by his own character to punish evildoers. These were universal constants, applying equally to God's people and to foreigners. At the same time, the prophets were certain that God remained committed to his covenant people. His punishments were discipline, intended to correct and purify. When the time of punishment passed, a glorious future would burst upon the world. God's great delight was in blessing human beings, not in causing pain, even when punishment was called for. Ultimately, God is Love in the Old Testament as well as in the New. And ultimately, God will bless.

The LORD your God wins victory after victory and is always with you. He celebrates and sings because of you, and he will refresh your life with his love.

Zephaniah 3:17 CEV

Something to Ponder

The Major and Minor Prophets provide a consistent picture of the future. As history's end approaches, God will bring his people back to the Promised Land (Isaiah 11:11–12; 43:1–8; Jeremiah 16:14–16; Hosea 1:10–11; Amos 9:11–15). There will be a terrible war in the Middle East (Ezekiel 38–39; Isaiah 30:31–33; Joel 2:1–17), after which the Messiah will appear to establish and rule an everlasting kingdom (Isaiah 4:2–6; Jeremiah 31:1–27; Daniel 2:31–45; Joel 2:26–32). Some people take these images figuratively. But should we take them literally, there is no doubt that a consistent common view of the future emerges.

Digging Deeper

Locusts were the scourge of the ancient Middle East. These grasshopper-like insects multiplied rapidly and formed swarms that literally cast a dark cloud over hundreds of square miles. One locust swarm that passed over the Red Sea in 1899 was estimated to cover two thousand square miles! When the locusts alighted, they devoured every  bit of living vegetation. They often laid eggs, and when the eggs hatched, the larvae would consume new growth as they emerged. Along with drought, locusts were among the most feared natural phenomenon of the ancient world.

Prophets After the Exile—
Haggai, Zechariah, and Malachi

The prophets who ministered in Judah foresaw the destruction of Judah. They also predicted a return to Judah of captives in Babylon. So it is no surprise that forty-two thousand Jews returned in 538 BC. Their story, told in the historical books of Ezra and Nehemiah, is filled with discouragement. Jerusalem was a heap, little Judah's villages lay in ruins, and once-fertile fields were overgrown with brambles. After laying the foundation for a new temple, the people focused on clearing fields and providing homes for themselves. The temple project was set aside until conditions improved.

Haggai

On August 29, 520 BC, the prophet Haggai preached a sermon that energized the little community. Within the first eleven verses of the first chapter of his book, Haggai announced that the Jews had not prospered because they failed to put God first. The leaders and people responded. The whole community came together to build on the temple foundation laid eighteen years earlier.

> Is it time for you yourselves to dwell in your paneled houses while this house lies desolate?
>
> Haggai 1:4 NASB

> The LORD God will save them on that day, because they are his people.
>
> Zechariah 9:16 CEV

On October 17, 520 BC, Haggai had a word of encouragement for the Jews. God was with them in their efforts. But how could an impoverished community find the funds to build and beautify the temple? The answer is found in Ezra 6:8–12. Although the governor of their province opposed the rebuilding, the king of Persia ordered the governor to finance the entire project!

Haggai preached again on December 18 to share God's promise, "from this day on I will bless you" (Haggai 2:19 NIV). And on the same day, Haggai spoke to Zerubbabel, a descendant of David, to reaffirm the promise that one day a Davidic king would rule in Jerusalem.

Zechariah

In October 520 BC, Zechariah joined Haggai in urging the Jews to return to God and complete the temple. In February 519 BC, he was given the visions recorded in chapters 1-6.

Zechariah's major contribution, however, is his look ahead. Earlier, Daniel had visions of the world empires that would control the Holy  Land until the Messiah came. Zechariah's difficult-to-interpret visions looked at this era from the point of view of Jews living under Gentile rule in one of the 120 provinces of the mighty Persian Empire, and his visions gave insight into God's purposes.

The material in chapters 9-14 provides insights into God's intervention in history during the Messiah's first and second comings. The key to understanding these chapters is to note that they adopted a sophisticated literary form known as *chiasmus*, in which themes were balanced and set against each other.

The picture given in these chapters balanced judgment against salvation and portrayed the victories won by the coming Messiah in his roles as Shepherd of his people and as coming King. Despite the subservient role that God's people would have to play for centuries, in the messianic age all God's promises would be fulfilled, and the whole world as well as Israel would be blessed.

Malachi

Haggai and Zechariah mark a high point in the experience of the returned exiles. The people listened to God's messengers and responded. But some hundred years later when Malachi ministered, the people had grown indifferent to God and had drifted into various sins. For historical background, read Nehemiah 13.

Malachi is the last book of the Old Testament, and it draws a dismal portrait of the people's spiritual condition. When Malachi confronted his contemporaries, they responded with disdain and indifference. Accused of despising God's name by offering crippled or diseased animals as sacrifices, the people shrugged, complaining that worship was boring and a burden. The priests failed to teach God's law. And the people complained that God failed to answer their prayers, never considering that the callous ways they replaced their wives with younger and more beautiful trophy wives reflected their own indifference to covenant relationships. In this setting God announced, "I hate divorce" (Malachi 2:16 NIV).

> For you who fear My name, the sun of righteousness will rise with healing in its wings.
>
> Malachi 4:2 HCSB

When God urged the people through the prophet to return to him, they pretended shock, asking what the prophet meant. Return? Yet their indifference to religion and their priorities were clearly revealed by their failure to pay the tithe (10 percent of the crops of the land and the increase of their flocks) to support temple worship and the priesthood.

At the end of Malachi's book, it is clear that there was no hope for the restoration of the kind of faith-community envisioned in the Old Testament, and the prophet focused on individuals "who feared the LORD" and "talked with each other" about him (Malachi 3:16 NIV). God promised, "They will be mine . . . in the day when I make up my treasured possession" (verse 17 NIV).

Myth Buster

Many assume that Old Testament predictions of a return of the Jews to the Holy Land were fulfilled in 538

BC. But the same themes—of scattering throughout the nations and of a miraculous return to the homeland—are also found in these postexilic prophets. After the Romans destroyed Jerusalem in AD 70, the Jewish people were scattered again. Many view the establishment of the State of Israel in 1948 as evidence that the ancient prophecies about Israel will be completely fulfilled—perhaps even in our day.

Prophecies of Jesus in Zechariah

Prophecy of Event	Scripture
Jesus' entry riding a donkey into Jerusalem on Good Friday	Zechariah 9:9
Cheers of the crowd	See Matthew 21:1-11
Sale of the Messiah for thirty pieces of silver, the price of a slave	Zechariah 11:13
Silver's use for the purchase of a potter's field	See Matthew 26:14-16; 27:1-10
Arrest of Jesus and the fleeing disciples	Zechariah 13:7; see Matthew 26:47-56
Future return of Jesus as King over all the earth	Zechariah 14:9

The New Testament

The Old Testament prophets fell silent about four hundred years before Jesus. Then, with his advent, a new generation of spokespersons for God appeared with an old yet stunning new message.

Contents

The Centuries Between the Testaments 157

Life and Worship in the Holy Land 159

Jesus, Hero of the New Testament 161

Major Events in the Life of Jesus.. 163

From Holy Land Faith to World Religion 165

Peter, Paul, and the Apostles... 167

Grace, the Open Secret of Christianity.............................. 169

The Spread of the Gospel.. 171

In those days John the Baptist came, preaching
in the Desert of Judea and saying, "Repent,
for the kingdom of heaven is near."

Matthew 3:1–2 NIV

The Centuries Between the Testaments

More than four hundred silent years passed between the writing of Malachi and the birth of Jesus. During those years, no prophet appeared to reveal more of God's plan. Empires came and went; millions lived brief lives and then died. The world waited for an empire to weld nations and peoples together, equip them with common language, and offer them freedom to travel. When the conditions were just right, God acted. A child was born in Bethlehem, a town in insignificant Judea on the eastern edge of the Roman lands. The child was God's own Son.

In the Wider World

Two developments were critical in preparing for the New Testament era. The first was the conquests of Alexander the Great. Although Alexander's empire shattered into four parts on his death, the ruler of each segment carried forward Alexander's vision of a world unified by Greek culture and language. By the first century, ordinary people everywhere, in the far English Isles as well as throughout Europe and Asia Minor, spoke a common Greek language as well as their own national tongue.

In the decades before Jesus' birth, Rome had defeated every competing power and mastered the Mediterranean world. Roman roads linked major cities; Roman warships controlled the seas; Roman governors oversaw affairs in every part of Rome's vast empire. *Pax Romana*, a peace imposed by Rome under its greatest emperor, Augustus, guaranteed individuals freedom to travel and freedom of religion unknown in previous eras.

> When we were utterly helpless, Christ came at just the right time and died for us sinners.
>
> Romans 5:6 NLT

> You are the foundation on which we stand today. You always save us and give true wisdom and knowledge.
>
> Isaiah 33:6 CEV

During most of the four centuries between the completion of the Old Testament and the birth of Jesus, little Judea was squeezed between competing empires established by two of Alexander's generals, the Ptolemaic in Egypt, and the Seleucid in what had been Persia. Judea had known a semblance of self-rule under the Maccabees, a family that led a revolt against the Seleucids in 146 BC. But the last of the Maccabees willed his lands to Rome. By the time Jesus was born, Rome controlled the Holy Land through its puppet king, Herod the Great. At last conditions were right for God's next, decisive move.

Final Thoughts

The true significance of world events is best understood long after they take place. Looking back, we can often see a divine purpose hidden at the time.

Check Your Understanding

- **What is one major event that shaped the New Testament world, and why was it important?**

The spread of Greek culture was a major event that shaped the New Testament world. The spread of Greek culture meant that everyone spoke a common language, the language in which the New Testament was written and the good news was spread.

- **What other major event shaped the New Testament world, and why was it also important?**

The other major event that shaped the New Testament world was the emergence of the Roman Empire. The Roman Empire maintained peace, and it provided freedom for individuals to travel throughout the entire Mediterranean world with the gospel.

Life and Worship in the Holy Land

As the first century dawned, most Jews in the Holy Land lived in Judea or Galilee. The elite resided in Jerusalem, a city of some twenty thousand, but the majority of the people lived in tiny villages. The people were subjected to heavy taxes. These taxes were imposed by Rome and King Herod, but additional taxes in the form of tithes were paid to the temple. Many people farmed rich men's fields, and the landowners took much of every crop. Add taxes on goods brought into a city or a petty ruler's lands, and most people earned barely enough to live. No wonder many yearned for the Messiah to appear.

Jewish Faith and Practice

From birth to death, daily life was ordered by Moses' law, as interpreted by the teachers of the Law that the Gospels call *scribes* or *rabbis*. The temple was the religion's focal point. Sacrifices were offered at the temple daily, and during important religious festivals Jewish pilgrims from all over the world swarmed Jerusalem along with the residents of Judea and Galilee.

> You have revoked God's word because of your tradition.
>
> Matthew 15:6 HCSB
>
> He came to His own, and those who were His own did not receive Him.
>
> John 1:11 NASB

Two major parties dominated the religious scene. The *Sadducees* were led by the wealthiest families and highest priestly officials. They viewed the writings of Moses as authoritative, questioned the existence of angels, and did not believe in resurrection. The *Pharisees* were members of a minority lay movement, but their piety and commitment to keeping every detail of the divine Law gave them great influence with the common people. The Pharisees accepted as authoritative the entire Scripture. They believed in angels and in the resurrection of the dead. But the Pharisees also held that an *oral law* given to Moses was embodied in previous rabbis' applications of *written law* ("tradition"), a practice Jesus rejected.

Politically, the Sadducees were relatively comfortable with Herod's and the Roman's rule, while the Pharisees were more like the Zealots, who agitated for a military uprising and overthrow of Roman authority. It is no wonder that the men and women of this world, crushed by poverty and sustained by the hope of a future divine intervention, looked eagerly for God's promised Messiah.

Final Thoughts

The pressures under which first-century Jews lived led them to focus on prophecies that portrayed the Messiah's victory over foreign enemies and glorious rule. Against this background, we can understand the enthusiasm with which the Jews initially greeted Jesus and their disappointment when it became clear he had no intention of overthrowing the Roman Empire.

Check Your Understanding

▪ **Why was life so hard for the Jews in Judea and Galilee?**

The Jews in Judea and Galilee were subject to crushing taxes that made survival difficult.

▪ **What characterized the Sadducees?**

The Sadducees were upper class, wealthy, and comfortable with Roman rule. They held that only the five books of Moses were authoritative, and they did not believe in angels or resurrection.

▪ **What characterized the Pharisees?**

The Pharisees were committed to holy living in accord with traditional interpretation of Old Testament law, and they resented Roman rule. They accepted the entire Scripture, and they believed in angels and resurrection.

Jesus, Hero of the New Testament

Time itself pivots on the life of one human being, born more than two thousand years ago to a teenage Jewish girl in a backwater province of the mighty Roman Empire. That empire has long expired. Succeeding civilizations have crumbled into dust. But the Man continues to be worshiped by billions who acknowledge him as the God who came to take on our nature, revealed himself to us, and through his death called us to a personal relationship with himself. The Old Testament's covenants and promises point forward to him. The New Testament lifts him up, not merely as our example, but as our one best hope.

Jesus the Man

There's no doubt that Jesus was human. He was born a baby, grew to adulthood in an obscure village, and emerged unexpectedly as an itinerant teacher. Like other men, he knew hunger and exhaustion. Like other men, he felt the pain of rejection. Like other men, he died, experiencing the most demeaning and agonizing of deaths inflicted in the Roman Empire, crucifixion. But then, unlike other men, Jesus returned to life! The New Testament says that he was "declared with power to be the Son of God by his resurrection from the dead" (Romans 1:4 NIV).

Jesus told him, "I am the way, the truth, and the life. No one comes to the Father except through Me."

John 14:6 HCSB

Scarcely for a righteous man will one die; yet perhaps for a good man someone would even dare to die. But God demonstrates His own love toward us, in that while we were still sinners, Christ died for us.

Romans 5:7–8 NKJV

Jesus, God the Son

Some seven hundred years before Jesus' birth, Isaiah 9:6 described the event, prophesying, "A child is born to us, a son is given to us" (NLT). Jesus' life as a man began in Bethlehem. His existence as God the Son had no beginning. John's Gospel states, "The Word was with God, and the Word was God" (John 1:1 NLT).

The Old Testament book of Genesis poses a problem. How can a God of love return humans, who are snared in sin, to himself? The New Testament provides the answer. God can win humans back by becoming human and paying the price of human rebellion himself.

That's why Jesus is the hero of the New Testament. In his person's perfect bonding of God with humanity, Jesus gave his life for us. He truly is our hero. We will live because he came and died.

Final Thoughts

It is true that Jesus was a good person and a good teacher. But he was far more than this. To make Jesus less than he is presented to be in the Scriptures, fully human and at the same time truly God, is to make him irrelevant to the Bible's story and to ours.

Check Your Understanding

- **How does the calendar testify to the significance of Jesus?**

Time is calculated from before and after his birth. BC is short for "before Christ." AD is short for anno Domini, "the year of our Lord."

- **How is Jesus the hero of the Bible's story?**

Jesus not only is its central figure, but he also came to reveal his love and to die for the sins of a rebellious humanity. Through his death, human beings are promised life.

Major Events in the Life of Jesus

Most of Jesus' life was lived in obscurity. He grew up in a small town in Galilee. He worked with his supposed father, Joseph, as a carpenter-builder. When Joseph died, in harmony with Jewish tradition Jesus became head of his family and responsible for his mother, brothers, and sisters. Nothing in his life as a pious first-century Jew seemed to set him apart from thousands of other young Jewish men of his time. Until, at around age thirty, a series of stunning events set him apart forever.

Authentication

John the Baptist stirred the Jewish people with a call to repent and prepare for the promised Messiah (Deliverer). When Jesus was baptized, a voice from heaven proclaimed him the Son of God. Not long after Jesus began to preach, he stunned the crowds with his teaching and accompanying miracles and healings. During this initial phase of his ministry, everyone recognized Jesus as special, anointed and empowered by Israel's God.

> We all know that God has sent you to teach us. Your miraculous signs are evidence that God is with you.
>
> John 3:2 NLT
>
> [Jesus] was declared the Son of God with power by the resurrection from the dead, according to the Spirit of holiness.
>
> Romans 1:4 NASB

Growing Opposition

But Jesus' apparent disregard for traditional interpretations of Old Testament law aroused opposition from the religiously conservative Pharisees. At the same time, the more liberal and politically sensitive Sadducees feared that Jesus might proclaim himself the Messiah and initiate a rebellion that would force the Romans to destroy the nation. Both groups began to undermine his popularity.

The Turning Point

By the end of Jesus' second year of ministry, it became clear that the people accepted him as a prophet but not as the Messiah. Jesus had fallen short of the crowds' expectations that the Messiah would expel the Romans and establish an independent Jewish state. From that point on, Jesus' popularity waned

Climax

Each of the Gospel writers focused on events leading up to Jesus' execution. Jesus was tried in a religious court and then brought to the Roman governor, who pronounced the death penalty. Jesus was crucified and buried. But on the third day he was raised from the dead.

Final Thoughts

It is the Resurrection that confirms Jesus' claim to be the Son of God and the promised Messiah. It is the Resurrection that forever sets Jesus apart from every other religious leader the world has known.

Check Your Understanding

- **Why did religious leaders come to oppose Jesus?**

Some leaders were offended by his disregard for traditional interpretations of Old Testament law. Some were afraid he would stimulate a disastrous rebellion.

- **What was the turning point in Jesus' ministry, and what was the climax of his life on earth?**

The turning point came when the people decided Jesus was a prophet but not the Messiah predicted in the Old Testament. Jesus' execution and his resurrection three days later climaxed his life on earth.

From Holy Land Faith to World Religion

Jesus' resurrection from the dead confirmed the claims he made during his years as a controversial figure in Judaism. Within a few months his disciples publicly proclaimed him, and thousands of Jews responded to their message. The newly converted formed a sect within Judaism, "the Way," distinguished by their conviction that Jesus of Nazareth, then present in heaven, was both Messiah and Son of God. As more and more were drawn to faith in Jesus, persecution developed. Jesus' followers were driven from Judea, but everywhere they went they told others about the Savior.

How It Happened

At first the message spread within the Jewish community. Then Peter was directed by an angel to share Jesus with the household of a Roman centurion, and the Roman, too, believed. In Antioch, many like him converted and formed the first predominantly Gentile church. From Antioch, a young Jewish Christian named Saul, or Paul, set out to spread the good news of Jesus throughout the Roman Empire.

> Let all the house of Israel know with certainty that God has made this Jesus, whom you crucified, both Lord and Messiah.
>
> Acts 2:36 HCSB
>
> I am eager to preach the gospel to you. . . . It is the power of God for salvation to everyone who believes, to the Jew first and also to the Greek.
>
> Romans 1:15–16 NASB

Paul's Missions Strategy

During the next twenty years Paul traveled to major cities throughout the empire. Paul took his message first to Jewish synagogues. There he made contact with men and women who were attracted to Judaism's vision of one God and high moral standards. Even where the Jews opposed him, Paul planted communities of

Christians who spread the good news of God's love to outlying villages. Paul was joined in spreading the gospel by Jesus' apostles and other itinerant evangelists and teachers. By the time of Paul's death in AD 68, Christianity had taken root throughout the empire.

Christianity, born in tiny Judea, had been transformed from a sect of Judaism into a world religion.

Myth Buster

We often assume that Jews in the first century lived primarily in Palestine. But centuries before Jews had been settled in the world's major cities by the Assyrians and Babylonians. Some suggest that as many as 10 percent of all city dwellers in the Roman Empire were Jews. The existence of these Jewish communities was the key to Paul's missionary strategy.

Check Your Understanding

- **What were the main themes in the first proclamation of the gospel message?**

The main themes first proclaimed in the gospel message were twofold: Jesus experienced resurrection, and he is the Messiah promised in the Scriptures.

- **How was Christianity viewed initially, and how did it then become a world religion?**

Christianity was viewed initially as a branch or sect of Judaism, which was distinguished by the belief that Jesus was both Messiah and Son of God. When non-Jews (Gentiles) began to believe in Jesus, Paul and others carried the message of the resurrected Savior throughout the Roman Empire.

Peter, Paul, and the Apostles

Even before Jesus began his teaching ministry, he chose a dozen men to be with him. The Twelve listened and observed all he said and did. Trained in this way, they were ready after the Resurrection to lead the community of faith. Members of the Twelve were responsible for producing the Gospels of Matthew and John that relate the story of Jesus' life. The Gospel of Mark is a compilation by John Mark of the apostle Peter's stories about Jesus.

The Twelve Apostles

In the Gospels, Jesus' first twelve followers are called the disciples ("learners"). In the Epistles, the Twelve and Paul are called apostles ("special messengers"). When not speaking specifically of the Twelve and Paul, disciple means "follower," and apostle has the sense of "missionary." After Jesus' death and resurrection, the twelve men who knew Jesus' most intimately were commissioned his apostles, the first leaders of the early Christian church. The three most familiar are the impetuous Peter, the unquestioned leader of the Twelve; and the brothers James and John.

We did not follow cunningly devised fables when we made known to you the power and coming of our Lord Jesus Christ, but were eyewitnesses of His majesty.

2 Peter 1:16 NKJV

Pass on what you heard from me . . . to reliable leaders who are competent to teach others.

2 Timothy 2:2 MSG

The Apostle Paul

Paul was a young Pharisee who originally was a virulent enemy of the new faith. On his way to Damascus with authority to arrest Christians,

Paul had a vision of the resurrected Jesus. Immediately, Paul began to preach the faith he had tried to stamp out. Years later, Paul was commissioned by God and the Antioch church to set out on a missionary journey. During the next twenty years, Paul traveled and established churches. Thirteen of his letters to churches and individuals are preserved as books of the New Testament. These and letters written by other apostles preserve their legacy, and today serve as authoritative sources of authentic Christian teaching and lifestyle.

Other Church Leaders

Many others shared leadership in the earliest church. Each local community had its elders who provided spiritual oversight. Believers like Priscilla and Aquila, mentioned in Acts, taught and planted additional churches. In Romans 16 Paul mentioned a number of men and women with whom he worked closely over the years. As the first generation of leaders grew old and died, a new generation—persons like Timothy and Titus and John Mark—emerged to carry on their mission.

Check Your Understanding

- **What does *apostle* mean, and who are the "official messengers" of Christianity?**

An apostle is an official messenger, commissioned to represent an important personage, as the apostles were to Jesus. Counted as the "official messengers" are the twelve disciples who were with Jesus during his years of ministry and also Paul, who was converted on the road to Damascus.

- **What did the apostles do, and what is their legacy?**

The apostles launched the early church, having listened to and observed Jesus during his earthly ministry. Their legacy to us is their teaching, which is preserved in our New Testament.

Grace, the Open Secret of Christianity

There were a number of reasons for the rapid spread of Christianity. Some of these were sociological. *Collegia*, small neighborhood social groups that served a number of purposes, were common in the Roman Empire. Christians met in small groups and assembled in "house churches," which seemed familiar and natural. Yet the basic reasons for Christianity's rapid spread were theological. Honoring the empire's official deities was more a political and public statement than an act of personal faith. And the popularity of the many Eastern "mystery religions" that claimed to provide special access to a foreign deity demonstrated a deep, unsatisfied spiritual hunger.

✳

Beliefs About the Afterlife

Inscriptions on Greek and Roman tombs of the first century display a pervasive sense of despair. The person who died went to a dreary and empty realm, lost forever to loved ones. There was no hope, no prospect of a future for the dead. Then the gospel came, with its focus on a Man whose own resurrection offered hope to everyone who believes in him. As Paul reminded Thessalonian believers, their loved ones have simply "fallen asleep." Believers grieve, but not as "people who don't have any hope" (1 Thessalonians 4:13 CEV).

[God] has saved us and called us to a holy life—not because of anything we have done but because of his own purpose and grace.

2 Timothy 1:9 NIV

You were saved by faith in God, who treats us much better than we deserve. This is God's gift to you, and not anything you have done on your own.

Ephesians 2:8 CEV

Beliefs About the Gods

Greek and Roman deities inhabited their own realm and tended to ignore humans. One might gain the favor of a god or goddess, but the deities were capricious. Greek myths are full of stories of humans whose relationship with the gods brought disaster rather than blessing. Then the Christians came with a stunning revelation. The true God, the Creator of heaven and earth, loves each individual. He even took the initiative by reaching out in the Person of his Son, and went so far as to die for humankind's sins. Everyone who believes in the Son is welcomed into the family of God as a child and heir. At heart it is this unmerited favor—this grace—that set Christianity apart from all other religions and won the allegiance of the first-century world.

Final Thoughts

The sociological factors involved in the spread of Christianity are less significant than the theological. The appealing message of Christianity is that God loves human beings. He seeks a personal relationship with us that is based on what he has done for us rather than on what we can do to earn his favor.

Check Your Understanding

- **What was one sociological factor that aided the spread of Christianity?**

An important sociological factor that aided the spread of Christianity was the previous existence of collegia, small neighborhood groups, which made Christian house churches seem natural and familiar.

- **What are two theological factors that aided the spread of Christianity?**

The two theological factors that aided the spread of Christianity were: (1) The prospect of resurrection was appealing to those who had no hope for lost loved ones; and (2) the nature of God as a loving, caring Person who is moved by grace to save human beings was attractive.

The Spread of the Gospel

The New Testament contains three types of literature. There is biography: The New Testament begins with four portraits of Jesus. There is history: The book of Acts describes the spread of Christianity during the thirty years from just after Jesus' resurrection to about AD 63. And there are epistles: Letters of instruction and encouragement were written by early church leaders including the apostles Paul, Peter, and John.

Introducing Jesus the Christ

The purpose of the four Gospels is to introduce Jesus to the people of the first-century world. These are biographies written with particular audiences in view. Matthew intended to demonstrate to the Jews that Jesus fulfilled Old Testament prophecies concerning the Messiah. Mark wanted the Romans to see Jesus as a man of action. Luke wanted the Greeks to see him as the ideal human being. And John, writing much later, was concerned that everyone realize Jesus is first and foremost the Son of God.

After you have read this letter, pass it on to the church at Laodicea so they can read it, too.

Colossians 4:16 NLT

This is why I have sent to you Timothy, who is my beloved and faithful child in the Lord. He will remind you about my ways in Christ Jesus, just as I teach everywhere in every church.

1 Corinthians 4:17 HCSB

Sketching Early Church History

The book of Acts traces the stunning explosion of the church from a movement within Judaism to a world religion. Two men are selected by the writer, Luke, as central to his story. Peter, the leader of the apostles, was central in the early Acts story of the predominantly Jewish church. Paul was central in the story of Christianity's rapid expansion in the Gentile world.

Letters of Instruction and Encouragement

Paul's mission strategy called for planting churches in major cities of the Roman Empire and then moving on. He kept in touch with those churches through follow-up visits, visits from his associates, and correspondence. Typically, Paul's and others' letters deal with misunderstandings of Christian faith and lifestyle. Those letters were copied and circulated among the churches, and they quickly became recognized as authoritative. Today as well as in the early church, the New Testament Epistles (letters) are considered Christianity's foundational documents, the source and measure of Christian truth.

Final Thoughts

The New Testament documents emerged within a generation of the time of Jesus and stimulated the spread of Christianity. The Gospels' images of Jesus, the brief history of the church contained in Acts, and especially the Epistles' teachings and instruction, provided a firm foundation for the new faith.

Check Your Understanding

- **What three kinds of literature are found in the New Testament, and what is special about them?**

The three types of literature found in the New Testament include biography (the Gospels), history (Acts), and letters written by the apostles to the churches (the Epistles). All three types of literature were recognized as authoritative. The letters were copied and circulated. Today they serve as the source and measure of Christian truth.

- **Who are the central figures in the history book, Acts?**

The central figures are Peter, who was a leader among the apostles, and Paul, whose strategy was instrumental in planting churches.

The Gospels

The focus of the New Testament is on one unique individual, Jesus.
His significance is seen in four distinctive biographies, all written
within decades of his life, death, and resurrection.

Contents

Why Four Accounts of Jesus' Life? 175

Matthew—The Gospel of the Servant King 177

Mark—Portrait of a Man of Action..................................... 181

Luke—The Gospel of the Ideal Man.................................. 183

John—The Gospel of the Son of God................................ 187

Jesus performed many other signs in the presence of His disciples that are not written in this book. But these are written so that you may believe Jesus is the Messiah, the Son of God, and by believing you may have life in His name.

John 20:30–31 HCSB

Why Four Accounts of Jesus' Life?

The heart of the Christian message is reflected in the first recorded Christian sermon. Peter told a Jerusalem crowd, "This Jesus God has raised up" (Acts 2:32 NKJV). Peter's listeners all knew "this Jesus." Most knew someone he had healed or had heard him teach. All had heard stories and debated his identity. But as the message of a resurrected Savior spread beyond the Holy Land, "this Jesus" wasn't known. So the apostles and others told stories about him; stories that enabled others to become familiar with "this Jesus" too. Four collections of stories quickly were recognized as authorized biographies, recognized as true accounts of Jesus' life.

The Synoptic Gospels

Three of the accounts of Jesus' life are in chronological order. Matthew, Mark, and Luke follow Jesus from his emergence as a public figure through his crucifixion and resurrection. Two accounts, Matthew and Luke, include birth stories. Not surprisingly, the same stories are often found in two or even all three of these Gospels. Yet the stories are told with a different audience in view and often have different emphases.

Matthew's stories were told for a Jewish audience, to show that Jesus fulfilled Old Testament prophecies of the Messiah. In Matthew's Gospel, Jesus is King of a unique expression of God's eternal kingdom here on earth as well as Savior.

Since I have investigated all the reports in close detail, starting from the story's beginning, I decided to write it all out for you, . . . so you can know beyond the shadow of a doubt the reliability of what you were taught.

Luke 1:3–4 MSG

These are written that you may believe that Jesus is the Christ, the Son of God, and that by believing you may have life in his name.

John 20:31 NIV

Mark's stories were told for a Roman audience. The Romans, a practical people, admired strong and decisive men of action. Mark's shorter stories and faster pace presented Jesus in this light.

Luke's stories were written for a Greek audience. The Greeks, fascinated by the concept of the ideal, were shown a uniquely human Jesus who was concerned for the poor and for society's outcasts. Luke's Jesus set a new and different standard of excellence.

John's Gospel

Portraits of Jesus would be incomplete without a universal perspective. Jesus is more than Messiah, more than an incomparable man of action and ideal human being. Jesus is God the Son. And so there is a fourth Gospel, with stories and teaching not organized chronologically but organized around seven of Jesus' miracles. John's theme is that Jesus is divine.

Check Your Understanding

- Why were written biographies—the Gospels—of Jesus important to the church, and why were different ones written?

The Gospels were important to the church because the message had spread to many who, unlike his contemporaries in Judea and Galilee, did not know Jesus. Four different Gospels addressed different audiences—the Jewish audience (Matthew), the Roman audience (Mark), and the Greek audience (Luke)—as well as one written with a universal appeal (John).

- What are "Synoptic" Gospels, and which Gospels fit in this category?

Synoptic Gospels tell Jesus' story in chronological order. The Gospels of Matthew, Mark, and Luke are Synoptic.

Matthew—The Gospel of the Servant King

Writing his *Ecclesiastical Histories,* Origen stated that "the first Gospel was written by Matthew, who was once a tax collector, but who was afterward an apostle of Jesus Christ, and it was prepared for converts from Judaism." There's no doubt Matthew was written for a Jewish audience. This Gospel contains fifty-three quotes from, and seventy-six additional allusions to, the text of the Old Testament. Matthew wanted his Jewish readers to understand that Jesus was the promised Messiah, even though he proved to be a servant King.

Born a King

Matthew opens with a genealogy and the story of Jesus' birth. The genealogy demonstrates Jesus' credentials as a descendant of King David. In the story, Matthew quoted or referred to Old Testament prophecies, whose context presented the Messiah as Israel's deliverer, victor over Israel's enemies, and ruler-to-be of God's kingdom on earth.

> "They shall call His name Immanuel," which translated means, "God with us."
>
> Matthew 1:23 NASB
>
> Seek first his kingdom and his righteousness, and all these things will be given to you as well.
>
> Matthew 6:33 NIV

It is a bold opening. For the fact is, Jesus did not go to war with Israel's oppressors or establish an earthly kingdom. The remainder of Matthew's Gospel explains why.

Two Contrasting Visions

The Old Testament contains two contrasting visions of the Messiah. In one he is an all-powerful deliverer. In the other he is the Servant of the Lord (Isaiah 42–49) who was rejected by his own people and suffered death for them (Isaiah 53). It is understandable that first-century inhabitants of Judea and Galilee, suffering under oppressive rule, focused on the first vision. But then, after the death and resurrection of Jesus, Matthew's task was to present Jesus as the suffering servant and to answer the question, What happened to the Messiah's kingdom?

Matthew's Answer

We see Matthew's answer to the questions rightly posed by the Jewish community as we walk through his Gospel and note the themes of succeeding chapters.

Within the flow of Matthew's argument are many familiar and wonderful passages that merit special comment.

The Beatitudes (Matthew 5:3–12)

This series of statements highlights conflicting values. According to Jesus, it is better to be "poor in spirit" (Matthew 5:3 NKJV) (humble) than to be self-confident and self-reliant. It is better to mourn and turn to God for comfort than to be pleasure-seeking and hedonistic, always skating on

the surface of life. It is better to be meek than proud, powerful, and important. It is better to hunger for righteousness than to go through life satisfied with less. And it is better to be merciful than to be self-righteous and judgmental.

At first this catalog of attitudes seems peculiar. We prefer pleasure to mourning, and we admire the self-confident more than the humble. But each attitude Jesus encouraged focuses our attention on God, while the contrasting values implied focused attention on ourselves. Jesus' point was that nothing can bring greater satisfaction than to be close to God.

The Lord's Prayer (Matthew 6:9–13)

Jesus taught this prayer, which is repeated weekly in many churches, to his followers to teach them how to pray.

The phrase "Our Father" (Matthew 6:9 NKJV) teaches us that our relationship with God as our Father is the basis for confidence that God hears our prayers. But God is no earthly father. God is "in heaven" (6:9 NKJV), the Master of the universe. Because his power is unlimited, he is able to answer our prayers.

> Whoever wants to become great among you must be your servant. . . . just as the Son of Man did not come to be served, but to serve, and to give His life—a ransom for many.
>
> —Matthew 20:26, 28 HCSB

At the same time, we remember that his name is to be "hallowed" (6:9 NKJV). We are aware we are in the presence of the awesome Being who created all things. The phrase "your kingdom come" (6:10 NKJV) acknowledges that God's priorities rightly come first. When we say "your will be done on earth as it is in heaven" (6:10 NKJV), we commit ourselves to choosing his will daily, whether his answer to our prayer is yes, no, or not yet.

Each phrase teaches us more about prayer.

Themes in the Gospel of Matthew

Theme	Chapters
Jesus fulfills prophecy, qualifies as the Messiah.	1–4
Jesus requires the inner transformation of citizens of his kingdom; this must come first.	5–7
Jesus' authority over all is established by his miracles.	8–11
As opposition to Jesus hardens, he describes a mystery form of God's kingdom to be established on earth.	12–15
Jesus is rejected as Messiah, though honored as a prophet; this is the theological turning point in Matthew's Gospel.	16–17

Themes in the Gospel of Matthew (cont'd)

Theme	Chapters
Jesus exemplifies servanthood, which is the key to greatness in his present kingdom.	18–20
Jesus exposes opponents' motives, denounces them.	21–23
Jesus will establish the earthly kingdom predicted in the OT, but not until he returns.	24–25
Jesus dies and is resurrected, fulfilling prophecies about the suffering Messiah.	26–28

Dictionary

Messiah *(n.)* The long-awaited King of the Jews.

Digging Deeper

The Gospels report thirty-one different miracles. The miracle stories often show Jesus' compassion and concern for human beings. In Matthew 8–11, however, miracles are organized in a sequence that displays Jesus' authority over disease (8:1-14), demons (8:28-34), nature (8:23-27), sin (9:1-13), and death itself (9:18-26). These miracles support Matthew's argument that Jesus must be the promised Messiah.

Mark—Portrait of a Man of Action

About AD 140, Papias identified John Mark (Acts 12:25; 13:5, 13; 15:36–41) as the "interpreter of Peter" who recorded events in this Gospel "with great accuracy, but not, however, in the order in which it was spoken or done by our Lord." What Mark did was shape his storytelling to capture the imagination of Roman readers, who admire decisive, authoritative men of action. Mark immediately recounted miracles that established Jesus' authority over illness, demons, nature, and death itself (Mark 1:14–5:43). Jesus was a Person no reasonable Roman dared ignore.

The Audience

It is clear that Mark wrote for a Roman audience. He was careful to explain Jewish practices, and he translated Jewish terms into Roman equivalents (Mark 2:18; 7:3-4). He constantly used the word *immediately* when describing events. The Jesus of Mark's Gospel is vigorous, strong, and decisive. Mark avoided theological terms and speculation; he simply presented Jesus to his readers, confident that having met Jesus, each would realize that Jesus could not simply be ignored.

Everyone . . . kept saying to each other, "What is this? It must be some new kind of powerful teaching! Even the evil spirits obey him!"

Mark 1:27 CEV

Do not be amazed; you are looking for Jesus the Nazarene, who has been crucified. He has risen.

Mark 16:6 NASB

Themes in Mark

After telling the miracle stories that establish Jesus' authority, Mark described Jesus' conflicts with the religious leaders (Mark 6:1-8:26) and then his instruction of his disciples (Mark 8:27-10:52). Every great

Roman faced and overcame opposition and gathered followers around him. But then Mark plunged into the events leading to Jesus' death on the cross and his resurrection. Fully a third of the Gospel is devoted to Jesus' final week (Mark 11–16), for this is the core of Mark's story. Jesus seemed to experience an utter defeat . . . but God transformed his shameful death on the cross into history's greatest triumph. Jesus, now "the Lord Jesus," was "taken up into heaven and sat down at the right hand of God" (Mark 16:19 HCSB), the place of ultimate authority and power. Jesus' victory is complete.

Final Thoughts

Roman society emphasized the relationships of great men, "patrons," and their "clients" who owed them allegiance. Romans reading Mark would have viewed Jesus as the ideal patron. In this sense, Mark constituted a strong appeal to his readers to make a personal decision to seek a relationship with Jesus.

Dictionary

crucifixion *(n.)* 1. Death by suspension on a cross, arms stretched out above, hands nailed to the crossbar, causing blood to drain to the lower body, lungs to heave, pulse rate to increase. 2. A shameful and agonizing death, reserved in ancient Rome for slaves and the worst of criminals. 3. A slow death, often taking days.

Luke—The Gospel of the Ideal Man

Luke's Gospel is the longest book of the New Testament. The early church believed that Luke, like Acts, was written by the physician who accompanied Paul on several missionary journeys (Colossians 4:14; 2 Timothy 4:11). This tradition is supported by the many references to illnesses and descriptions of cures in the two books. Luke probably wrote his Gospel while Paul was imprisoned in Caesarea about AD 58, giving Luke the opportunity to speak with eyewitnesses and conduct the careful investigations he describes in Acts 1:1.

The Greek Ideal

Greek culture held up the ideal of excellence, the perfection of the individual physically, morally, and intellectually. Yet that ideal man was essentially self-centered and self-absorbed. In presenting Jesus to the cultured people of the first century, Luke displayed an individual who selflessly dedicated himself to serving God and others.

I have not come to call the righteous, but sinners, to repentance.

Luke 5:32 NKJV

The Son of Man has come to seek and to save that which was lost.

Luke 19:10 NKJV

Distinctive Themes

Luke followed the same chronological approach as Matthew and Mark. While much in Luke overlaps those two Gospels, most of the material in Luke 9–19 is unique, including six miracles and eighteen parables. Among the familiar material related only by Luke are stories of the good Samaritan and the prodigal son.

Luke highlighted Jesus' relationships with people from every strata of society. His emphasis on women is striking, particularly in view of the suspicion with which religious Jews of Jesus' time viewed women. When Luke's stories contrasted a man and a woman, the woman was invariably cast as the more admirable. One example: When an angel announced the birth of John the Baptist to the priest Zacharias, he doubted and was struck dumb (Luke 1:5-25). When an angel told the unwed Mary she would bear the Savior, she rejoiced (Luke 1:26-56).

Luke Emphasized Jesus' Human Touch

As we skim through this Gospel, we see Luke's repeated emphasis on the humanity of Jesus:

As a boy of thirteen, Jesus was so caught up in talking about his Father with respected teachers of God's law, he was stunned that his parents were upset when they finally found him after discovering his absence (Luke 2:41-52).

While teaching in an unnamed town, a man "covered with leprosy" appealed to him. Jesus reached out compassionately and touched the man before cleansing him of the disease (Luke 5:12-14).

The Pharisees, hoping to accuse Jesus of "working" and thus breaking the Law, planted a man with a withered hand in a synagogue where Jesus was teaching on the Sabbath. Jesus knew what they were thinking, but he healed the man anyway. The Pharisees were furious, and they began to plot how to get rid of Jesus (Luke 6:11).

When an expert in biblical law tried to avoid the command to love God and neighbor by challenging, "Who is my neighbor?" Jesus told the story of the good Samaritan who risked attack by robbers to help an injured Jew. The point, that any person in need, whatever his race or religion, is our neighbor, stunned the expert (Luke 10:25-37).

One Sabbath Jesus saw an obviously distressed woman who had suffered from an issue of blood for eighteen years. He called her over and healed her. The ruler of the synagogue was indignant that Jesus had "worked" in his synagogue on the Sabbath! Jesus rebuked him as a hypocrite for his lack of compassion, humiliating his enemies but delighting ordinary people (Luke 13:10-17).

When tax collectors and "sinners" flocked to hear Jesus, the religious leaders were scandalized. They would never associate with such people! But Jesus told the story of a lost sheep the shepherd searched for, and he called his friends to rejoice on its recovery. In the same way, heaven rejoices when a lost sinner is found, a truth that drives Jesus to befriend the outcasts of society (Luke 15:1-7).

> Everyone . . . kept saying to each other, "What is this? It must be some new kind of powerful teaching! Even the evil spirits obey him."
>
> Mark 1:27 CEV
>
> Do not be amazed; you are looking for Jesus the Nazarene, who has been crucified. He has risen.
>
> Mark 16:6 NASB

The night before his crucifixion, Jesus prayed alone on the Mount of Olives. He was in such anguish that "his sweat was like drops of blood falling to the ground " (Luke 22:44 NIV). But when the betrayer Judas led a mob to the hillside to drag him before a court packed with his enemies, Jesus spoke to them calmly and went unresisting to his fate (Luke 22:39-53).

This is the Jesus whom Luke presented: a compassionate, brave, caring Man who was committed to revealing his Father's character as a God of love.

Remember that while he was still in Galilee, he told you, "The Son of Man will be handed over to sinners who will nail him to a cross. But three days later he will rise to life" (Luke 24:7 CEV).

Myth Buster

Luke 8:27-38 tells about Jesus' casting a legion of demons out of a man of Gerassa into a herd of pigs. Matthew 8:28-34 tells what appears to be the same story, but in Matthew there are two men and they are from Gadara. A discrepancy in Scripture? Archaeology has shown that the same area was known as both Gerassa and Gadara in Jesus' day. And the fact that two men were present needn't keep Luke from focusing on

just one of them. It is wise when we find an apparent error in Scripture to withhold judgment until we have all the facts.

Sightings of the Resurrected Jesus

People Who Saw Jesus	Scripture
Mary Magdalene, near his tomb	John 20:1–2
Mary Magdalene and Mary the mother of James, near his tomb	Matthew 28:6–8
Two disciples, on the Emmaus Road	Luke 24:13–31
Disciples minus Thomas	Luke 24:36–45 John 20:19–24
Seven disciples, by the Lake of Tiberias	John 21:1–23
Five hundred, in Galilee	1 Corinthians 15:6
Paul, on the road to Damascus	Acts 9:3–6 1 Corinthians 15:8
Stephen, when he was stoned	Acts 7:55
Paul, in the temple	Acts 22:17–19 Acts 23:11
John, on the Isle of Patmos	Revelation 1:10–3:22

John—The Gospel of the Son of God

John wrote his Gospel in the last quarter of the first century, half a century after Jesus' death and resurrection. The story of Jesus was familiar then, spread by the Gospels of Matthew, Mark, and Luke. So, rather than retell the story, John focused on the significance of Jesus. In John's own words, he wrote that "you will put your faith in Jesus as the Messiah and the Son of God. If you have faith in him, you will have true life" (John 20:31 CEV).

A "Different" Gospel

Skim quickly through John's Gospel, and differences from the three Synoptic Gospels are immediately clear.

Matthew and Luke began with accounts of Jesus' birth. John took us back before the beginning of time, when God the Son existed with God and as God. God the Son, whom John calls the Word, the agent of creation, the very source of life and light, entered the world he made and presented himself to his own (John 1:1-11).

The three Synoptic Gospels walked us through Jesus' ministry from its beginning to the Resurrection. John selected seven miracles that led to extended teaching by Jesus. Most events related in the Synoptics took place in Galilee. John focused on events that took place in Judea.

God loved the world so much that he gave his one and only Son, so that everyone who believes in him will not perish but have eternal life.

John 3:16 NLT

Most assuredly, I say to you, he who hears My word and believes in Him who sent Me has everlasting life, and shall not come into judgment.

John 5:24 NKJV

The three Synoptic Gospels simply presented the Savior. John viewed Jesus through the lens of contrasting theological concepts: belief/unbelief, life/death, light/darkness, love/hate, truth/falsehood. Through it all, John's central concern was *belief*, a word that occurs ninety-eight times in the Greek text of John's twenty-one chapters.

Only John gave a lengthy account of what Jesus taught at the last supper he shared with his disciples the evening before the Crucifixion (John 13–16) or reported Jesus' final prayer for his followers (John 17).

Different Gospels, Same Jesus

The differences between John and the three Synoptics raise an important question. Is John's stress on the deity of Jesus consistent with the portrait of Jesus in the other Gospels? John cast Jesus as "equal with God" (John 5:18 NIV). He said that Jesus claimed to be the I AM, the God of

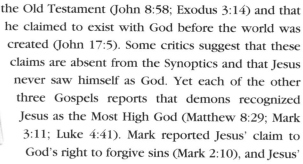

the Old Testament (John 8:58; Exodus 3:14) and that he claimed to exist with God before the world was created (John 17:5). Some critics suggest that these claims are absent from the Synoptics and that Jesus never saw himself as God. Yet each of the other three Gospels reports that demons recognized Jesus as the Most High God (Matthew 8:29; Mark 3:11; Luke 4:41). Mark reported Jesus' claim to God's right to forgive sins (Mark 2:10), and Jesus' claim to deity was one of the charges brought against him at his trial (Matthew 6:63–65). The differences between the Synoptics and John's approach in his Gospel can't cloud the fact that the same Jesus is presented to us in each; a Jesus whose miracles demonstrated his unique authority, and whose resurrection showed him to be the Son of God (Romans 1:4).

Jesus' "I Am" Statements

John reported a number of claims Jesus made using an intensive construction translated "I am." In using this construction, Jesus identified himself with the I AM (the God, Exodus 3:14) of the Old Testament. As

God, Jesus claimed to have come down from heaven (John 6:41, 51). He claimed to have existed before Abraham was born (8:58). Jesus claimed to be the gate through which one must enter to be saved (10:9). As the way, the truth, and the life, Jesus claimed to be the sole avenue through which a person might come to God (14:6).

Reading John's Gospel

When reading John's Gospel, be alert for passages that contrast light with darkness, life with death, truth with falsehood, love with hate, and belief with unbelief. Other key terms in John's Gospel and his letters are *word* (focusing on expression and communication), *world* (as human society), and *know* (often meaning "experience"). Also note that lengthy passages often begin with a question Jesus was asked. His first, brief answer puzzled his hearers, so Jesus then provided the lengthy explanation. It is also important to note that Jesus' teachings in John called for a faith response from his original hearers—and from us as well.

> I am the resurrection and the life. He who believes in Me, though he may die, he shall live.
>
> John 11:25 NKJV

Something to Ponder

Jesus told an inquiring religious leader he must be "born again" (John 3:3 NIV). The phrase *born again* has become a touchstone for evangelical Christians. But what did Jesus mean? Faith in Jesus not only gives the believer new, spiritual life (John 3:16), but also makes him or her a part of God's family (John 1:12–13). God becomes "our Father who is in heaven" (Matthew 6:9 NASB), and we become children of God (1 John 3:1).

Digging Deeper

The writers of the New Testament invented a new grammatical construction to express what they meant by "believing" in Jesus. Biblical faith involves far more than believing *that* Jesus lived and died, and far more than our beliefs about him. So the early Christians used the preposition *en* in conjunction with *believe*, a construction Greek scholars today call the "mystical dative." To believe in Jesus involves a personal investment in what we know of him. To believe in Jesus means to rely on his promises and to rest the full weight of our hope on the salvation God offers us in him.

Myth Buster

Today some claim that the notion Jesus is divine, the unique Son of God, is an invention of his disciples. It is interesting, then, in John's Gospel, and in the other Gospels as well, to note a peculiar reaction to Jesus by the religious leaders. There were many "brands" of Judaism in the first century. While these differences generated heated arguments, none moved adherents, intent on murder,

to tear up the cobblestones from the streets to use as weapons. But this occurred more than once when Jesus spoke of his identity (John 8:59; 10:31). When Jesus asked which teaching the leaders intended to stone him for, they answered that it wasn't his teaching. It was because he, a mere man, was claiming to be God. If you take the Gospel accounts at all seriously, you have to admit the statement that Jesus never claimed to be God just doesn't hold up. His most bitter enemies didn't believe his claim. But they had no doubt he made it.

Acts, Letters, and Revelation

After Jesus' resurrection, the Christian message spread quickly across the Roman Empire. Important leaders in the early church wrote letters that appear in the New Testament, which closes with a mysterious book named Revelation.

Contents

Acts—Growth of the Church 193

Romans—The Solution 195

1 Corinthians—The Problem-Solving Epistle 197

2 Corinthians—New Covenant Ministry 201

Galatians—Faith and Freedom 203

Ephesians—Understanding Jesus' Church 205

Philippians and Philemon—Praise from Prison 209

Colossians—The Real Jesus 211

1 and 2 Thessalonians—Look Ahead Eagerly 213

1 and 2 Timothy and Titus—Letters to Young Leaders 217

Other Early Church Leaders 221

Hebrews—The Superiority of Jesus 223

James—Faith That Works 227

1 Peter—Suffering Saints 229

2 Peter—Against Heresy 233

1 John—Experiencing Daily Fellowship with God 235

Jude—Contending for the Faith 239

Revelation—The Final Triumph 241

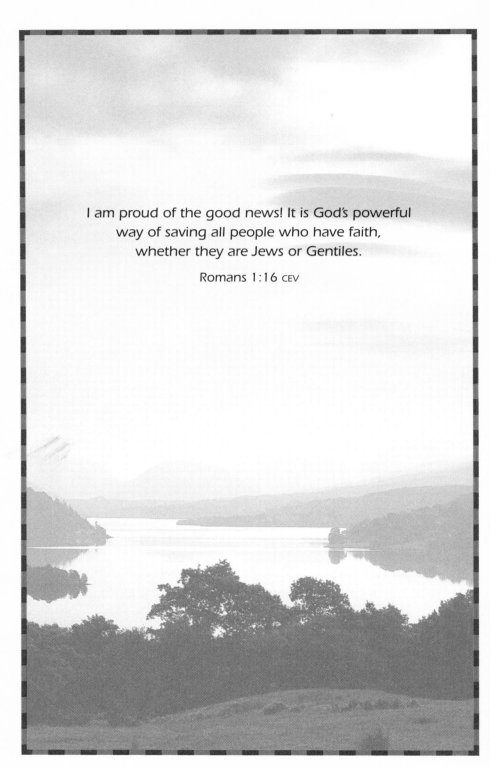

I am proud of the good news! It is God's powerful
way of saving all people who have faith,
whether they are Jews or Gentiles.

Romans 1:16 CEV

Acts—Growth of the Church

The apostle Paul is the predominant figure in the New Testament. The book of Acts, after a brief account of the growth of the church in Jerusalem, focuses on Paul and his missionary journeys. It introduces us to the cities where Paul founded churches, cities that later were the recipients of the letters that compose his "books" of the New Testament. These books establish Paul as Christianity's premier theologian as well as its most famous missionary.

Paul's Letters

It isn't that Paul's purpose in penning the New Testament books that bear his signature was to write theological treatises. Paul was writing letters; letters that contained warm expressions of affection, practical advice, rebuke, and exhortation.

Often Paul referred to things he taught members of the young churches when he was with them, clarifying misunderstandings or reminding them of points he'd made in person. Several of the letters were written to individuals; three were written to younger leaders filled with advice, and one was written to an older believer about a runaway slave.

> All Scripture is inspired by God and is profitable for teaching, for rebuking, for correcting, for training in righteousness.
>
> 2 Timothy 3:16 HCSB
>
> Be imitators of God, therefore, as dearly loved children and live a life of love, just as Christ loved us and gave himself up for us.
>
> Ephesians 5:1–2 NIV

The theological content was typically woven through the letters, leaving it to later Christians to piece together systematic presentations of Christian faith. Yet Paul's letters touch on all the central elements of Christianity. Romans and Galatians focus on the salvation God provided to believers and on salvation's impact on daily life as well as man's eternal future. Ephesians provides insight into the nature of the Christian community; Colossians provides insight into the person of Jesus and his centrality.

In answering questions raised by the Thessalonians, Paul's reply presented fresh insight into the return of Jesus and the link between Christianity and Old Testament prophecy. Even when Paul responded to practical questions about problems experienced in Corinth, his answers tended to be based on his understanding of God and what God was doing.

Final Thoughts

By weaving Christian teaching into his epistles, Paul failed to present a systematic account of Christian faith. But Paul's approach has significant advantages. In the personal give-and-take characteristic of letters, we are given a clear vision of how Christian faith impacts the daily lives of believers.

Check Your Understanding

- **In what two roles did the apostle Paul excel?**

The two roles in which Paul excelled were as a missionary—to Rome, Galatia, and Ephesus, among other places—and as a theologian.

- **What type of literature are the New Testament books Paul wrote, to whom did he write, and what are the implications of his writing style?**

Paul's New Testament books are all epistles, personal letters. They were written either to communities of believers (churches) or to individuals. Paul did not develop a systematic exposition of Christian doctrine, but he did demonstrate the implications of Christian truth for believers' lives.

Romans—The Solution

The Bible's story begins with a puzzle. How can sinful human beings, in persistent rebellion against God, be forgiven and a personal relationship with God be reestablished? As century follows century, it is clear that God forgives and accepts sinners. But on what basis? It was left to the apostle Paul, Christianity's greatest theologian as well as its most effective missionary, to explain. In Romans, Paul showed that all of Christianity hinges on the death and resurrection of Jesus and on what that death and resurrection meant.

Tracing the Argument

Paul took the theme of righteousness and carefully developed it in Romans. By tracing his arguments, we come to understand God's solution to the problem of human sin and rebellion.

Humans have abandoned God and are under God's wrath. Scripture says, "There is none righteous, no not one" (Romans 3:10 NKJV). God chose to credit us with righteousness as a gift. Sins past, present, and future may all be forgiven on the basis of Jesus' sacrifice.

> God raised Jesus to life! God's Spirit now lives in you, and he will raise you to life by his Spirit.
>
> Romans 8:11 CEV
>
> Fix your attention on God. You'll be changed from the inside out.
>
> Romans 12:2 MSG

God accepted Abraham's faith in place of righteousness. He did the same for David. Their experiences establish the principle that applies to all who trust God's promise of salvation in Jesus. Adam's disobedience corrupted our whole race, locking us in the grip of spiritual death. Jesus' obedience enabled God to provide us with the gift of eternal life.

We can now choose to let Jesus actually make us more and more righteous. The secret is surrendering to the Holy Spirit and letting the Spirit shape our attitudes and actions. Ultimately, at history's end, we'll be completely transformed into Jesus' likeness. God is at work fashioning a righteous community. The common goal of this new community is to nurture individual growth, to help one another respond to Jesus as Lord, and to worship as one glorifying God.

Paul expressed his desire to visit Rome, and he sent greetings to individuals who had partnered with him in spreading the message of Jesus.

Something to Ponder

Christian life remains a struggle. An inner pull toward what we know is wrong is at war with an honest desire to do what's right. All too often we have to say with the apostle Paul, "I do not do the good that I want to do, but I practice the evil that I do not want to do" (Romans 7:19 HCSB). The good news is that Jesus is present to strengthen us.

Digging Deeper

The message of the book of Roman's has had a lasting impact on Western Christianity. It was the conviction that God's righteousness is shared with humans by faith and through faith that motivated Martin Luther, the founder of the Lutheran Church and initiator of the Reformation. And it was while listening to a reading from Luther's commentary on Romans that John Wesley, the founder of the Methodist Church, felt his heart "strangely warmed" and was converted.

1 Corinthians—The Problem-Solving Epistle

The apostle Paul's missionary strategy was to share the gospel's good news, teach new believers, and then move on to another city. It is not surprising that problems cropped up in the young churches or that people wrote to Paul for advice. In this first letter to the Corinthians, Paul provided guidance on a number of important issues that had shattered the unity of the Corinthian believers, forcing them into different camps. Paul solved these divisive problems by providing perspective rooted in basic Christian truth. He then applied the truth to show how the church can act to restore unity.

Conflict Resolution

Hurts, disagreements, and conflicts are still common in the community of faith. Christians are human, and the happenings in the Corinthian church of Paul's day are all too familiar. Paul's first letter to the Corinthians helped the church resolve many of their conflicts. And Paul's letter is relevant today, not because we have to deal with exactly the same issues, but because Paul demonstrated an approach to conflict resolution that we can adopt.

> Christ knows, and we have Christ's Spirit.
>
> 1 Corinthians 2:16 MSG
>
> Whether, then, you eat or drink or whatever you do, do all to the glory of God.
>
> 1 Corinthians 10:31 NASB

His approach was simple but profound: (1) Paul identified a problem behavior. (2) Paul evaluated the cause of the behavior. (3) Paul identified a perspective that believers should adopt. (4) Paul described the changed behavior that would result.

Looking at a couple of the problems Paul dealt with in 1 Corinthians, we can see how Paul's approach worked.

Divisions in the Church (1 Corinthians 1:10–4:21)

The problem. Some people identified themselves by allegiance to super-star leaders like Paul, Apollos, or Peter. This created division.

The cause. The Corinthians were thinking like mere men. They needed to adopt God's perspective (wisdom) as shared through the written Word.

The new perspective. Human leaders are God's servants, filling different roles. The Corinthians needed to focus on "God, who makes things grow" (1 Corinthians 3:7 NIV) and stop boasting about favorite leaders.

The changed behavior. The Corinthians should respect and appreciate Christian leaders but no longer "take pride in one man over against another" (1 Corinthians 4:6 NIV).

Dispute over Dinner (1 Corinthians 8–10)

This problem was more complex than the division caused by believers' aligning themselves with different leaders. But Paul's approach to resolving the conflict remained essentially the same.

The problem. The main source of meat was sacrificed animals. If one wanted a steak dinner, he went to a temple meat market. The trouble was, the animal had been sacrificed to a pagan god. Some Christians saw eating this meat as participating in idolatry. They were critical when other Christians, who dismissed pagan gods as fictional, freely ate meat whenever they wished. And those who felt free to eat looked down on their fellow believers as superstitious and foolish.

The cause of the problem. The believers tried to resolve differences by applying their knowledge of Christian doctrine. The result was that each side got puffed up, sure it had it "right." They needed to approach this issue by looking to love, not knowledge, for love would open up each side to the Holy Spirit's teaching.

The new perspective. They needed to stop arguing about who was right and consider how to show love to their fellow believer. They would not want their example to cause a "weak" brother (who was convinced it was wrong to eat the meat) to violate his conscience.

The changed behavior. Believers needed to do what was loving, even if they had to give up meat: (1) A big deal shouldn't be made about giving up the "right" to meat. Apostles surrendered their rights all the time; but (2) they did stay away from idolatry. Demons masqueraded as pagan gods, and immorality had always been associated with idolatry. And (3) if believers were taken to dinner by a non-Christian, they should go ahead and enjoy their steak. But if their host made a point of saying the meat was dedicated to a god, they should not eat it for the sake of their host's conscience. Finally, (4) whatever they chose to do, they should do it to glorify God, and in love they should consider others' welfare.

> Watch, stand fast in the faith, be brave, be strong. Let all that you do be done with love.
>
> 1 Corinthians 16:13–14 NKJV

For Personal Study

You can use this four-step analysis to better understand Paul's teaching in 1 Corinthians. When you're not sure about anything Paul said, you might refer to a Bible handbook. A Bible handbook will typically trace the New Testament writer's argument. Best of all, when you face a conflict or a problem in your own local church, you can often restore unity by following Paul's approach to conflict resolution.

Digging Deeper

Corinth was destroyed in 146 BC but rebuilt in 46 BC. The Corinth Paul knew was a center of trade and the capital of Achaia, with a population of some 250,000. The city was infamous for loose living and sexual immorality. Many of the problems in the Corinthian church seemed rooted in the character of the city, even as problems in churches today reflect the moral climate of our society. The apostle Paul spent about eighteen months in Corinth between AD 50 and 52. This letter was written perhaps five years later.

Conflicts in Corinth

Issue	Chapters in 1 Corinthians	Resolution
Divisions	1–4	Focus on God; view human leaders as servants.
Church discipline	5	Ostracize persistent sinner.
Lawsuits	6	Let fellow believers settle the dispute.
Sexual immorality	6	Dedicate your body to God as his temple.
Sex in marriage	7	Relations in marriage are to be continued.
Eating meat	8–10	Deal with this by applying love, not knowledge.
Women at worship	11	Women are to participate.
Lord's Supper	11	Treat this rite with full respect.
Spirituality	12–13	The measure of spirituality is love, not one's gifts.
Gifts at worship	14	Give prophecy (teaching) priority.
Resurrection	15	Jesus' resurrection guarantees ours.

2 Corinthians—New Covenant Ministry

Paul's first letter to the Corinthians helped. Many there took his advice, and the problems were solved. Yet some continued to carp and criticize. So Paul penned this second letter. In it he shared the principles on which his ministry was based. Just as the notion that salvation and transformation are God's gifts seems strange to many people, Paul's ministry didn't fit with his culture's notion of leadership. But that was and is the point. Christian ministry is to derive its form from the gospel and from the truly peculiar way God works in human hearts.

Principles of Paul's Ministry

Be embarrassingly honest and open (1–3). Paul shared his fears and weaknesses. His kind of openness took boldness. Even Moses put on a mask to hide the fact that the splendor his face exhibited after meeting with God was fading. Paul removed masks, aware the Holy Spirit transforms believers "with ever-increasing glory" (2 Corinthians 3:18 NIV). Removing masks revealed weaknesses, but it also let people see the change Jesus was working.

> Our hope for you is firmly grounded, knowing that as you are sharers of our sufferings, so also you are sharers of our comfort.
>
> 2 Corinthians 1:7 NASB

> We do not focus on what is seen, but on what is unseen.
>
> 2 Corinthians 4:18 HCSB

Be confident, whatever the evidence to the contrary (4–5). That which can be seen is transitory. Only unseen realities are eternal. Paul didn't become discouraged when he heard of problems in Corinth. Through the gospel, Jesus had taken up residence in the Corinthians' hearts. It was unthinkable that God's purpose—to give new life that would be lived for him—should be thwarted. Deep within, Christians were new creations, and God was at work in even the most reluctant.

Be committed and ready to suffer (6–7). The great leaders of this world are praised. Jesus' apostles are persecuted. But serving other believers makes it all worthwhile.

Give freely, but not because you have to (8–9). The command to tithe no longer applied. Instead there was an invitation to trust God and respond generously to the needs of brother and sister believers.

Be powerless, yet wield authority (10–13). Christian leaders have no power to coerce. But Jesus speaks through them. Paul relied on Jesus' power to bring about obedience to his teaching.

Final Thoughts

The world's leaders demand and coerce. Christian leaders influence by example and by displaying confidence in God's ability to transform sinners into saints. Such leadership seems feeble rather than strong. But it takes a strong individual to lead the way Paul advises.

Something to Ponder

Second Corinthians 8–9 is the core New Testament passage on giving. Giving in the Old Testament began with the tithe, 10 percent of the produce of the land paid as "rent" to God as owner of the holy land. New Testament giving began with the recognition that 100 percent of what we have is God's. We are freed to give freely by the assurance that God is able to meet all our needs and that he is glorified when we use his gifts to meet the needs of others.

Galatians—Faith and Freedom

A persistent debate raged in the early church. Some were convinced that Gentile Christians should be responsible to keep Moses' Law. The apostle Paul insisted that Christians were not to relate to God through the Law at all. The issue came to a head at a council held in Jerusalem (Acts 15). But around AD 49, before the council met, Paul wrote this brief letter to Christians in Galatia. Paul had no doubts at all. Faith, not Law, frees us to live righteous lives.

Christians and the Law

The argument from experience (1-2). Paul went to Galatia with a gospel that God revealed to him. Faith in that gospel—not keeping the Law—had saved the Galatians. What's more, the Jerusalem apostles had affirmed Paul's gospel of faith in Jesus unmixed with law. Peter himself backed down when Paul confronted him for giving in to Jewish Christians who distorted the gospel by acting as if Gentile believers were second-class citizens.

> It is no longer I who live, but Christ lives in me; and the life which I now live in the flesh I live by faith in the Son of God, who loved me and gave Himself for me.
>
> Galatians 2:20 NKJV

> Only crazy people would think they could complete by their own efforts what was begun by God.
>
> Galatians 3:3 MSG

The argument from sacred history (3-4). Abraham's experience proved that faith has priority. Law, introduced hundreds of years later, could not nullify or replace the principle of faith. Besides, Scripture itself said law was a temporary expedient, to function only until the promised seed of Abraham appeared. Now that Jesus had come, Christians were adopted as sons. It's as if the Law were a nanny, in charge while children are young. In Jesus Christians were adopted and acknowledged as sons. Christians relate directly to the Father, not to the Father through the nanny.

The argument from transformation (5-6). Christians have both old and new natures. The old wants to sin, and when the Law says don't, the old nature experiences a surge of energy. The new nature is stirred up by the Holy Spirit, who is present in Christians' hearts and lives. There is no help for Christians in the Law, who have to look to the Holy Spirit, the only one who can make them loving, kind, patient, and peaceful persons.

Final Thoughts

Living by faith may not be easy. But it beats trying to rely on our willpower to do what the Law says is right. When we rely on our own efforts, we're not counting on God. Living by faith is the only way the Christian life really works.

Something to Ponder

What did Paul mean when he wrote, "It is for freedom that Christ has set us free" (Galatians 5:1 NIV)? Christian freedom is freedom to do what God wants as well as freedom to avoid responding to that urgent impulse to sin. Paul's letter to the Galatians reminds us that as long as we rely on our own efforts to break the hold of sin, we are in bondage. Only by relying on the Holy Spirit can we find freedom to live truly good and happy lives.

Ephesians—Understanding Jesus' Church

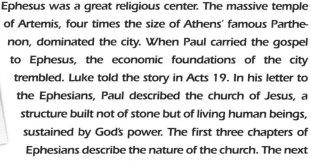

Ephesus was a great religious center. The massive temple of Artemis, four times the size of Athens' famous Parthenon, dominated the city. When Paul carried the gospel to Ephesus, the economic foundations of the city trembled. Luke told the story in Acts 19. In his letter to the Ephesians, Paul described the church of Jesus, a structure built not of stone but of living human beings, sustained by God's power. The first three chapters of Ephesians describe the nature of the church. The next three explore implications for Christian living. The nature of the church shapes the way we are to live together as believers.

What Is the Church? (Ephesians 1–3)

The church is God's creation (1:1-23). God took an active role in planning and providing forgiveness of sins. The forgiven are special to him, his own treasured possession. The church is the community of all the forgiven. One way God invites us to picture the church is as a living body, with each Christian intimately linked to all and with Jesus as the head and the source of the body's life.

> God is so rich in mercy, and he loved us so much, that even though we were dead because of our sins, he gave us life when he raised Christ from the dead.
>
> Ephesians 2:4–5 NLT

> By grace you are saved through faith, and this is not from yourselves; it is God's gift.
>
> Ephesians 2:8 HCSB

The church is revitalized humanity (2:1-10). God fashioned the church from people who once were spiritually dead. To create the church God gave such people spiritual life, not because of anything they did to deserve life, but simply out of love. The mark of this free gift is a faith in Jesus that is also God's gift.

The church is reconciled humanity (2:11-22). Jesus' sacrifice restored harmony between people and God; peace has replaced hostility. That is true, too, of Christians' relationships with others. Differences that once caused hostility and fear have been made irrelevant in view of the fact that believers are united in Jesus' body.

Paul introduced two images. We are now one body, and we are members of the same household. The bond between Christians is real and indivisible.

The church is an unexpected element of God's eternal plan (3:1-13). Paul paused to identify the church as a "mystery." *Mystery* is a technical theological term applied to some aspect of God's plan that was not revealed in the Old Testament. The older Scriptures did reveal that Gentiles would be saved (Isaiah 42:6; 49:22), but never hinted that Gentiles would be united with Jews as one people.

The church is God's family (3:14-21). Paul added another picture of what the church is. He pointed out that the church derives its identity from God the Father. Since he is our Father, we must be family. When Christians are "rooted and established in love" (Ephesians 3:17 NIV) for other family members, we experience the reality of God's love through our love for one another.

Loving makes "every effort" to maintain unity (4:1-6). This calls for humility and gentleness, putting up with ("bearing with," verse 2, NIV) each other as we focus on the essentials: "one Lord, one faith, one baptism, one God and Father of all" (verse 6, NIV).

Loving is ministering to one another, helping one another grow (4:7-16). God provided leaders to equip believers to minister to one another.

Loving is committing to a new and holy lifestyle (4:17-5:2). Paul said, "Be kind and compassionate to one another, forgiving each other, just as in Christ God forgave you" (Ephesians 4:32 NIV).

There is no place in a life of love for obscenities, debauchery, or sexual immorality.

Loving is being submissive to each other (5:21-6:9). Each person in a relationship is to demonstrate submission (essentially, responsiveness) in appropriate ways. Husbands demonstrate submission by loving their wives as Jesus loved the church, wives by being responsive to their husbands. Children demonstrate submission by obeying their parents, parents by not being hard on them. Slaves demonstrate submission by obeying their masters, masters by treating them with respect.

> Be imitators of God, as beloved children.
>
> Ephesians 5:1 NASB

God has equipped us for our life together as his church (6:10-20). As a Roman infantryman is fully equipped, so are Christians. We are equipped with truth, righteousness, and the gospel; and with salvation, faith, and the Word of God. With these weapons, Christians can stand against the most powerful of spiritual enemies.

Myth Buster

Read the word *church*, and many think "building" or "denomination." But *church* is never used this way in the Bible. In fact, Christians didn't meet in churches for at least the first 120 years of the Christian era. The Greek word translated "church," *ecclesia*, indicated an assembly of citizens called together to deal with public affairs. The  New Testament consistently views Christ's church as a people God has called together to worship him and to grow in their common faith. The message of Scripture, and especially of Ephesians, is that the church is *people*.

Digging Deeper

Ephesians 6:1 notes that the commandment to obey parents comes first and that it comes with a promise. This command isn't first in the list of ten in Exodus 20, but it is the first commandment any child has to deal with. The promise "that your days may be long on the land the Lord your God is giving you" (NIV) explains its significance. Only generations of Jews who obeyed God could count on a long life in the Holy Land, something many exiled Jews learned the hard way. A child who learns to be obedient and responsive to parents is more likely to be responsive to God as an adult. And only responsiveness to God can lead to his blessing.

Something to Ponder

Roman religion featured cold, public rituals. Like the massive stone temple in Ephesus, religion was sterile and empty. Christianity adopted and adapted a different social setting, the *collegia*. These were local associations of persons who shared an occupation or a neighborhood, and who banded together for mutual support and to pay funeral costs. But there was a radical difference between  the society's *collegia* and Christian house churches. The bond that united believers was a common commitment to Jesus Christ. And Christian *collegia* united people of different social classes who otherwise had nothing to do with one another. Paul stated the ideal that many early Christians lived out: "There is neither slave nor free, male nor female, for you are all one in Christ Jesus" (Galatians 3:26 NIV).

Philippians and Philemon—Praise from Prison

Acts ends around AD 62 or 63, with the apostle Paul imprisoned in Rome awaiting trial. While there he wrote several letters, commonly called the "Prison Epistles"— Ephesians, Colossians, Philippians, and Philemon. Only the last two make specific reference to his prison experience. Surprisingly, the key word in the longer letter, Philippians, is *joy*! In time, Paul was acquitted of all charges and released. He enthusiastically returned to his missionary work but was arrested later and, about AD 68, was executed in Rome. From his testimony in Philippians, we can assume that his last days there were also filled with joy.

Paul's Joy

If we underline each verse in which Paul spoke of his joy or rejoicing, we get a clear insight into the apostle. Joy bubbled up as he recalled the Philippians' sharing with him in the Gospel (Philippians 1:3-5). The realization that Jesus was being preached thrilled him, even though some evangelists had questionable motives (1:18). Looking ahead filled Paul with joy. Whether he lived or died, he won! (1:19-21). Paul urged the Philippians to complete his joy by being humble and likeminded (2:1-2), and the thought of his sacrifice for them would be another source of joy (2:17). And Paul rejoiced in God himself (4:4), as well as in recent indications of the Philippians' love for him (4:10).

Don't worry about anything, but pray about everything.

Philippians 4:6 CEV

Keep your minds on whatever is true, pure, right, holy, friendly, and proper. Don't ever stop thinking about what is truly worthwhile and worthy of praise.

Philippians 4:8 CEV

If Paul's happiness had depended on wealth or possessions, he might have been driven to despair. But Paul valued unseen realities, and nothing could rob him of his joy.

Jesus' Example

Philippians 2:5–11 is one of the key passages defining Jesus' identity. Paul reminded us that Jesus existed as God but surrendered the prerogatives of deity. He humbled himself to become a human being, and then further humbled himself by suffering a felon's death on the cross. But God raised Jesus up and exalted him, naming him Lord.

The passage has implications beyond theology. Living humbly may involve suffering, but God exalts the humble in the end.

Final Thoughts

Many people live in the pursuit of wealth or power or pleasure, and near life's end they realize they've never been truly happy. The apostle Paul reminded us in Philippians that by giving priority to the service of God and others, we can find joy whatever our circumstances may be.

Something to Ponder

Paul wrote to Philemon, the master of a runaway slave Paul met while in prison. The slave, Onesimus, had come to know Jesus, and Paul encouraged his old master to welcome him back, not just as a servant but as a brother in Jesus. Slaves made up some 50 percent of the population in many cities. Paul did not condemn the institution,  which was embedded in first-century civilization. He encouraged Christians to stop viewing their slaves as property, however, and to treat them as fellow human beings. We may not be able to change our world, but we can change the way we live in it.

Colossians—The Real Jesus

Imagine a world in which everything material is evil, and everything immaterial is good. Some people held that view and imposed it on the Christian message. To them, Jesus could not have been God. God, who is good, would have had nothing to do with the evil material world. He couldn't even have created it; some lower deity or angel must have done that. And surely a man dying on a wooden cross could have nothing to do with salvation! The result was that these folks, later called Gnostics, came up with a counterfeit Jesus and a counterfeit Christianity.

The Authentic Jesus (Colossians 1:3–2:15)

In Colossians, Paul confronted Gnostics' notions. Jesus is the exact representation ("image") of the invisible God (1:15). Visible and invisible realms were both created by Jesus—including those immaterial angels Gnostics worshiped (1:16). Only Jesus' power holds the universe together (1:17). What's more, Jesus' death in a flesh-and-blood body reconciled us to God. Only the death on the cross of the real Jesus, truly God and fully human, can give life to those who are spiritually dead and make them holy (2:13–15).

> In him all the fullness of Deity dwells in bodily form.
>
> Colossians 2:9 NASB
>
> Chosen by God for this new life of love, dress in the wardrobe God picked out for you: compassion, kindness, humility, quiet strength, discipline.
>
> Colossians 3:12 MSG

The Authentic Christian life (Colossians 2:16–4:18)

Gnostics had two views about daily life, each rooted in their belief that the material body is essentially evil. One view is ascetic: Since the body is evil, punish it. Hungry? Refuse the body food. The other view is hedonistic: Let your body do whatever it wants. Thirsty? Drink all the wine you want. What the evil body does has nothing to do with the real, immaterial *you* or your spiritual life.

Authentic Christianity insists that lifestyle counts. Christians are called to express God's character and values in the real world. We are to put aside anger, malice, and immoral living (3:1–9) and be compassionate, kind, humble, and forgiving in our relationships with others (3:12–16). Contrary to Gnosticism, Christianity has everything to do with the way we live in these bodies of ours. And how we live does count.

Final Thoughts

Jesus lived as a devout first-century Jew, daily observing the Law and showing concern for others. We live in a different world. Yet, as followers of Jesus we, too, are to be committed daily to doing what is right and showing a Christlike concern for others.

Digging Deeper

The Gnostics viewed knowing God as an intellectual exercise. Paul's prayer in Colossians 1:9–11 lays out a different path. We are to discover what God has willed (as revealed in Scripture) and apply it with all wisdom and insight in our daily lives. Thus we'll live worthy and productive lives and come to know God in a personal,  experiential way. As Jesus said, "If anyone loves me, he will obey my teaching. My Father will love him, and we will come to him and make our home with him" (John 14:23 NIV).

1 and 2 Thessalonians—Look Ahead Eagerly

Paul spent only a short time in Thessalonica and then was driven out of the city (Acts 17). But he succeeded in establishing a vital Christian community that spread the gospel to the surrounding countryside. Later Paul learned these new Christians were confused about his teaching on Jesus' return. He wrote them two letters laying out two core teachings concerning what lay ahead, and how God's revelation of the future would impact their lives.

1 Thessalonians

Each of Paul's letters to churches features passages encouraging his readers to live holy lives. That element is in 1 Thessalonians, too, along with the apostle's evident pleasure with the way the Thessalonians have received and are sharing the Word of God. But two sections of this first letter are unique and worthy of special attention.

Paul's personal relationships (2:1-12). Paul was in Thessalonica only a brief time. Yet he described his relationship with these people in the warmest of family terms. He had loved them as a mother loves her infant. And, like a caring father, he found time to be with each one, to instruct, encourage, and exhort

> You are waiting for his Son Jesus to come from heaven. God raised him from death, and on the day of judgment Jesus will save us from God's anger.
>
> 1 Thessalonians 1:10 CEV

> You know quite well that the day of the Lord's return will come unexpectedly, like a thief in the night.
>
> 1 Thessalonians 5:2 NLT

them to live lives worthy of God. Reaching out to others still requires loving them and sharing ourselves with them.

Jesus' promised return (4:13-5:11). Some of the Thessalonian Christians had died since Paul left. The others were concerned. Paul had taught that Jesus would come back. Had the Thessalonians' loved ones missed out on Jesus' return and on resurrection? Paul answered with a resounding no.

When Jesus comes back the Christian dead will come out of their graves. Together with living believers, they will rise to meet Jesus in the air, to be forever with God.

Paul's words encouraged the Thessalonians, and they encourage us. Yes, we sorrow when a loved one dies. But it isn't the inconsolable grief of those who have no hope of resurrection. We Christians know we will be reunited beyond the grave.

Paul said it could happen at any moment, so it's especially important to remain committed to living holy and loving lives (5:1-11).

2 Thessalonians

A few months later, Paul wrote again. Some of the Thessalonians were convinced that the persecution they experienced was evidence that the world was coming to an end (compare Matthew 24). Some even quit work and were sponging off other Christians.

Something must happen first (2 Thessalonians 2:1-12). This teaching is the core of Paul's response to the Thessalonians' questions. Before the world would end, the Antichrist (the "man of lawlessness" [2:23 NIV] predicted in Scripture) must appear to be utterly defeated at the reappearance of Jesus. True, the hostile spiritual forces that will animate this individual were at work in the world then. But there will be no mistaking the Antichrist when he appears.

Focus on the present in view of the future (2 Thessalonians 1:3-12; 2:13-3:14). How are believers to apply teaching about God's final victory? First, Paul told the Thessalonians to persevere despite persecution. God will vindicate his own and punish evildoers when Jesus returns (1:5-12).

Second, they were to stand firm and hold on to what they had been taught (2:13-17). Third, no one knows when the world will end (3:6-15). So the unemployed were to go back to work and focus on doing good.

Inconsistencies?

In 1 Thessalonians, Paul taught an imminent return of Jesus, one that could happen at any time, with no preconditions. But in 2 Thessalonians, Paul said that before the end, the "man of lawlessness" (2:3 NIV) must appear. Is this an error in Scripture, or at least an inconsistency?

> It is a righteous thing with God to repay with tribulation those who trouble you, and to give you who are troubled rest . . . when the Lord Jesus is revealed from heaven.
>
> 2 Thessalonians 1:6–7 NKJV

Not necessarily. Jesus' first coming spanned thirty-plus years. Why assume, then, that end-times prophecies must be squeezed into a brief period? In fact, Daniel's prophecy of the seventy weeks (Daniel 9:20-27) suggests that events at history's end will unfold over a period of seven years. In this case, there's no need to assume that the resurrection of Christians and their meeting Jesus in the air (an event called the *Rapture*) must happen at the same time as or after the appearance of the Antichrist.

Despite the fact that some teachers of prophecy create complicated charts supposedly showing the sequence of predicted events, no such charts are provided in Scripture.

Final Thoughts

What God does provide through glimpses of the future is encouragement, as in the case of sorrow at the death of loved ones, and exhortation to hold on to our faith when persecution comes.

Digging Deeper

Scripture is realistic about work. Sometimes work can be toil and drudgery. Yet work also has great value. First Thessalonians 4:11–12 notes that work keeps us from being dependent on others and wins the respect of others. Second Thessalonians 3:6–15 reinforces this thought: Work is not only the way we accept responsibility for ourselves, it is an essential source of self-respect. But Ephesians 4:28 makes the most important point: When we work, we not only can care for ourselves, but we can also gain resources to share with others in need. More than the wealth work earns, work provides opportunities to do good.

Basic Truths in the Letters to the Thessalonians

Even though Paul spent very little time with the Thessalonians, he was careful to ground them in basic Christian truths. This chart indicates basic truths that are mentioned in the two Thessalonian epistles.

Truth	Scripture
Inspiration and authority of Scripture	1 Thessalonians 2:13
	2 Thessalonians 2:15
	2 Thessalonians 3:6–17
Trinity	1 Thessalonians 1:1, 5–6
	1 Thessalonians 4:8
	1 Thessalonians 5:19
	2 Thessalonians 2:13
Deity of Jesus	1 Thessalonians 3:11–12
	2 Thessalonians 2:16–17
Jesus' sacrifice	1 Thessalonians 4:14
	1 Thessalonians 5:9–10
	2 Thessalonians 2:13–14

1 and 2 Timothy and Titus—Letters to Young Leaders

From the beginning, the apostle Paul traveled with a team. Among his team were seasoned elders like Silas and Barnabas. There were also younger men, like John Mark, Timothy, and Titus, whom Paul was grooming to lead the next generation of Christians. By the mid-sixties, it had become clear that the days of Peter, Paul, and the original twelve apostles were coming to an end. No wonder Paul packed urgent advice in his letters to Timothy and Titus. Humanly speaking, the future of the Christian movement was soon to be in their hands.

✳

Pastoral Epistles

The Pastoral Epistles is the name commonly given to Paul's letters to Timothy and Titus. Not that Timothy and Titus ever settled down to pastor a local church. Timothy and Titus became itinerant missionaries and troubleshooters, going from city to city to strengthen Christians and correct error. That was their role when Paul wrote the three letters, from about AD 64 through 67. Given that those young leaders had the same basic mission, it's not surprising that the topics Paul took up in the three letters overlap.

I am writing you these instructions so that, if I am delayed, you will know how people ought to conduct themselves in God's household, which is the church of the living God.

1 Timothy 3:14–15 NIV

What you have heard from me in the presence of many witnesses, commit to faithful men who will be able to teach others also.

2 Timothy 2:2 HCSB

Repeated Themes in the Pastorals

A common goal for Christian teaching. Each of the three letters opens with a reminder that the goal of Christian teaching is to produce believers who are motivated by godly and fervent love (1 Timothy 1:3–7;

2 Timothy1:3-12; Titus 1:1-4). The young leaders were urged to teach sound doctrine, not that knowledge of the truth is an end in itself, but that "the goal of our instruction is love from a pure heart, a good conscience, and a sincere faith" (1 Timothy 1:5 HCSB).

A common emphasis on living Christian faith. In each of the three letters, Paul reminded the young leaders of the need to "put religion into practice" (1 Timothy 4:12; 2 Timothy 4:1-5; Titus 2:1-15). Throughout the Epistles, there is a consistent link between sound doctrine and godly living. Thus Paul urged Titus to "insist that the people follow [these teachings], so that all who have faith in God will be sure to do good deeds" (Titus 3:8 CEV).

It is striking to note that in Titus Paul insisted "you must teach what is in accord with sound doctrine" (2:1 NIV). The chapter goes on to focus not on doctrines but on the appropriate way of living that Titus was to "teach," "train," and "encourage." It's clear from these Pastoral Epistles that *orthopraxy*, living the way Christians ought to live, is as significant as, and is derived from, *orthodoxy*, believing what Christians ought to believe.

A common view of local Christian leadership. Paul devoted sections of each letter to a discussion of local church leadership. A full chapter of 1 Timothy was devoted to discussing the qualifications of local leaders. In 2 Timothy, Paul described how a local leader was to live, teach, and correct (2:22-26). In Titus, Paul focused on the leader's example and duties (1:5-16).

> As for you, speak the things which are proper for sound doctrine.
>
> Titus 2:1 NKJV

When we compare these passages, the emphasis on the local leaders' character and example is striking. Paul didn't mention training or spiritual gifts as primary qualifications. Rather, he identified character traits that make the leader a positive example of a mature Christian.

Character Sketch of a Christian Leader

> The overseer must be above reproach, the husband of but one wife, temperate, self-controlled, respectable, hospitable, able to teach, not given to drunkenness, not violent but gentle, not quarrelsome, not a lover of money. (1 Timothy 3:2–3 NIV)

A common stress on the importance of being an example. In each letter, Paul reminded the young leaders of the importance of setting an example (1 Timothy 4:12–16; 2 Timothy 3:10–17). Timothy was not only to "command and teach" Christian faith and life, but must "set an example for the believers in speech, in life, in love, in faith and in purity" (1 Timothy 4:11–12 NIV). This is an emphasis found in other epistles as well. Paul could honestly hold himself up as an example, too, telling the Philippians, "Whatever you have learned or received or heard from me, or seen in me—put it into practice. And the God of peace will be with you" (Philippians 4:9 NIV). It's not enough to teach the truth. The teacher must model the truth as well.

Digging Deeper

An additional common theme, emphasized in the letter to Titus, is that of "good works." Christians sometimes are ambivalent about good works, concerned that if we emphasize works, some will imagine salvation depends on what we do rather than on what Jesus did for us on the cross. Paul's response was that "those who have trusted in God may be careful to devote themselves to doing what is good" (Titus 3:8 NIV). Good works flow out of our trust in Jesus and are an expression of that trust.

Something to Ponder

Despite the common threads, there are differences among the Pastoral Epistles. In 2 Timothy, written just before Paul's death, he envisioned troubled times ahead. Rather than the establishment of God's kingdom through the church, Paul foresaw a deteriorating society filled with self-absorbed, money-hungry, and self-promoting people who are "treacherous, ruthless, bloated windbags, addicted to lust, and allergic to God" (2 Timothy 3:4 MSG). Christians could expect persecution and opposition with courage and faith. The persecution Paul foresaw did come, and it still exists in many parts of the world.

Dictionary

orthodoxy *(n.)* System of belief that emphasizes what Christians ought to believe.

orthopraxy *(n.)* System of belief that emphasizes how Christians ought to live.

Final Thoughts

In a sense, the Pastoral Letters are Paul's "last words," a summary of what he had learned about ministering to others. Like anyone's last words, Paul's thoughts on Christian love, Christian lifestyle, and true Christian leadership are worth pondering.

Other Early Church Leaders

The most prominent leaders of the first generation of Christians were the twelve apostles, Jesus' original disciples, and Paul. Uncertain traditions trace the ministries of most of the Twelve, but with the exception of the apostle James, who was executed early on in Jerusalem, and Peter and John, Scripture provides no clues as to their ministries. Yet there were others whose roles are described or hinted at in the New Testament. As the decades passed, many, men and women alike, emerged to ensure the Christian message was spread throughout the Roman world and beyond.

Influential Men and Women

Barnabas and Silas were among men who played significant roles in the early church. Barnabas was the first to risk welcoming Paul, a notorious persecutor of Christians, after his conversion (Acts 9:20–27). Later he and Paul led the first Gentile church in Antioch, and Barnabas accompanied Paul on his first missionary journey. On another journey, Paul was joined by Luke, who traveled with Paul for years and wrote both the Gospel that carries his name and the book of Acts.

[God] Himself gave some to be apostles, some prophets, some evangelists, and some pastors and teachers, for the equipping of the saints for the work of ministry, for the edifying of the body of Christ.

Ephesians 4:11–12 NKJV

God works in different ways, but it is the same God who does the work in all of us. A spiritual gift is given to each of us so we can help each other.

1 Corinthians 12:6–7 NLT

Other leaders are less familiar. Apollos, who preached repentance, learned of Jesus from Priscilla and her husband, Aquila (Acts 18:18–28). Phoebe was commended as "a leader in the church at

Cenchreae" (Romans 16:1 CEV). And of course there were young Timothy and Titus, Paul's troubleshooters. The progress of Christianity rested on their shoulders as well as the shoulders of the apostles. Some played even more significant roles.

The General Epistles

The letters in the New Testament that were not written by the apostle Paul are called the General Epistles. Two were written by Peter, and three were written by John. Perhaps surprisingly, other letters weren't written by apostles. James and Jude wrote the books that bear their names. We don't know who wrote Hebrews. Speculation about the author has led to suggestions that Hebrews was written by Barnabas, Apollos, or perhaps Priscilla. Though authorship remains a mystery, the book's place in Scripture is secure.

Final Thoughts

The less-familiar names in Scripture, and the inclusion of books in the New Testament not written by an apostle, remind us that in every generation God raises up leaders for his church. He might even be raising up you.

Check Your Understanding

- **What are the General Epistles, and who wrote them?**

The General Epistles are New Testament letters that were not written by the apostle Paul. Three of the General Epistles were written by authors who were not among Jesus' original disciples: James, Jude, and the unknown writer of Hebrews.

- **What is the significance of 1 Corinthians 12:6–7?**

"God works in different ways, but it is the same God who does the work in all of us. A spiritual gift is given to each of us so we can help each other" (NLT) means that you are a significant person in Jesus' church.

Hebrews—The Superiority of Jesus

The book of Hebrews was written to Christian Jews. In the first century, for a Jew to accept Jesus meant ostracism from the larger Jewish community. Christian Jews were cut off from temple worship and the festivals they'd known from childhood. Some considered returning to the familiar ways. God had ordained the life Jews lived. As the pull to return to Judaism became stronger, an unknown writer who knew the Old Testament intimately picked up a pen to write a letter that would help Jewish believers realize just what they had in Jesus.

✳

It's All About Relationship

The focus of Old Testament law was on personal relationship with God. The rules laid down by God on Mount Sinai set standards God's Old Testament people had to live by to remain in fellowship with him. But God was fully aware of human frailty, and so the Law provided priests to represent sinners before God. It provided blood sacrifices to atone for, or cover, sins. For spiritually sensitive Jews, God's law provided for continuing, intimate relationship with the Creator.

> We do not have a high priest who is unable to sympathize with our weaknesses, but One who has been tested in every way as we are, yet without sin.
>
> Hebrews 4:15 HCSB

Hebrews, Too, Is All About Relationship

The writer of Hebrews understood Old Testament law and the blessings it conferred. But the writer understood something else. The Old Testament system was inadequate. It was a temporary expedient because God had always intended to replace it. The replacement would be a system that could guarantee full and complete forgiveness and even provide for transformation of sinners into godly men and women.

A Superior Revelation (Hebrews 1:1–4:13)

The Jews believed angels mediated the giving of God's law to Moses. The writer introduced Jesus as the Son of God and thus far superior to angels (1:1–14), although he was also a true human being (2:1–18). The writer also argued that Jesus, as the owner of God's house, is superior to Moses, who received the Law. Moses was a great man, but he was only a servant in God's household (3:1–6).

The writer then went on to warn against failing to listen to Jesus (3:7–15). It was vital that his readers pay close attention to the surpassing revelation they had been given by God's Son.

A Superior High Priest (Hebrews 4:14–8:13)

Once a year, Israel's high priest entered the Holy of Holies in the temple to make a sacrifice that covered the sins the nation had committed during the past year. But Jesus entered heaven itself with a sacrifice that provided forgiveness for all sins—past, present, and future! Unlike Israel's high priest, Jesus lives forever to guarantee access to the Father (Hebrews 7:24–28).

What's more, Jesus is High Priest of a new covenant. The Old Testament itself predicted that a new covenant would supplant the old, inadequate covenant God made with Israel through Moses (Jeremiah 31:31; Hebrews 8:1–13). Under the new covenant, the external standards imbedded in the Law are written on the believer's heart, making moral transformation possible.

A Superior Sacrifice (Hebrews 9:1–10:39)

Repeated sacrifices of the blood of bulls and goats covered sins temporarily, but it was impossible for such sacrifices to take sins away (10:1–4). Jesus' sacrifice of his own blood "once for all" (Hebrews 10:10 NIV) "perfected forever" (10:14 NIV) those who believe in him.

Jesus Provides for Our Sanctification (Hebrews 11:1–13:25)

The experience of Old Testament saints demonstrated the power of faith to change lives (Hebrews 11). And God was actively involved in the process of making those who had faith holy, disciplining and training them the way parents discipline their children. In closing, the writer of Hebrews urged his fellow Jewish Christians to keep on loving one another and remain committed to what they had been taught about Jesus.

Priesthood

Priests played an important part in Old Testament religion. When a person sinned the priests represented his interests, pleading with God for forgiveness and offering the required sacrifices. The priests presented God's concerns to the people, teaching what he expected from them. The most important priest was the high priest, who was the only one who could offer the special sacrifice on the Day of Atonement. The New Testament presents Jesus as our High Priest. Hebrews says he offered his own blood as the one sacrifice that could clean all of humanity's sins. As High Priest, Jesus is an advocate for us in heaven today.

He doesn't need to offer sacrifices every day, as high priests do—first for their own sins, then for those of the people. He did this once for all when He offered Himself.

Hebrews 7:27 HCSB

Every priest goes to work at the altar each day, offers the same old sacrifices year in, year out, and never makes a dent in the sin problem. As a priest, Christ made a single sacrifice for sins, and that was it!

Hebrews 10:11–12 MSG

Dictionary

sanctification (*n.*) 1. The state of being made holy. 2. In the New Testament, holiness through the sacrifice of Jesus (past), the new covenant (present), or transformation at the second coming of Jesus (future).

Digging Deeper

Angels fascinate many believers. Hebrews 1:14 describes them as "spirits sent to serve people who are going to be saved" (CEV). Angels were created by God before the material universe, and they do not die. There are many references to angels' appearing to humans in the Bible, and some people today report visits from angels. Angels are more powerful than humans. But as Hebrews reminds us, "Jesus clearly did not come to help angels, but he did come to help Abraham's descendants" (Hebrews 2:16 CEV). Abraham's descendants, not angels, are the focus of God's concern.

Myth Buster

Many people believe that the Old Testament simply isn't relevant today. But the book of Hebrews calls that position into question. Looking back into the Old Testament, the writer not only drew truth from its stories, but even found vital insights into Christian faith in Old Testament institutions and practices. In a real sense, the Old Testament is filled with shadows cast by the light that now shines in the New Testament's fuller revelation. And when we examine the shadows, when we see, for example, the function of the Old Testament sacrifices or the role of the Old Testament priest, we can see even more clearly the significance of the role of Jesus Christ in our own faith. The book of Hebrews reminds us that the Bible is one book, not two and not sixty-six. And every part of this great book can speak to us today.

James—Faith That Works

Martin Luther, whose rediscovery of salvation by faith alone launched the Reformation, was uncomfortable with the book of James. To Luther, James's emphasis on the practical difference faith should make in how we live was too close to the idea that salvation is something humans earn. But James wasn't writing about salvation. He was writing about the experiences of those who are already believers. And his concern was that the way believers live be in harmony with their beliefs. For James, faith that didn't make a difference wasn't faith at all!

The Problem Passage (James 2:14–26)

Two phrases troubled Luther: "Faith by itself, if it does not have works, is dead" (James 2:17 NKJV); and "A man is justified by works, and not by faith only" (James 2:24 NKJV). James was contrasting two kinds of faith, however: a faith that exists as a response to God's promise and that transforms our lives; and a faith that, like the devil's, is merely acknowledgment of God's existence. It is important to note that in this passage, *justified* is used in its legal sense as "vindicated." The truth of God's announcement that Abraham's faith was credited to him as righteousness and Abraham's claim to be a believer was demonstrated by the way Abraham lived his life.

> God will bless you, if you don't give up when your faith is being tested. He will reward you with a glorious life, just as he rewards everyone who loves him.
>
> James 1:12 CEV
>
> The seed whose fruit is righteousness is sown in peace by those who make peace.
>
> James 3:18 NASB

Simply put, James's point was that authentic faith is a dynamic transforming thing that by its very nature will change the way we live.

James's Concerns

The rest of this brief epistle looks at believers' lifestyles. James pointed out inconsistencies and challenged his readers to bring their lives into harmony with the faith they professed. In the process, James answered important questions: How should I understand and respond to temptation? What is "true religion"? What is the "royal law" that should guide my relationships with others? Why is it so important to guard my tongue? What should be my response to unfair treatment by others?

Final Thoughts

The book of James is filled with reminders that God expects Christians to be different in positive ways. It simply is not fitting to show favoritism, or to say mean and biting things about others. Nor is it fitting to be critical and judgmental. God and our neighbors should expect better things from followers of Jesus.

Something to Ponder

Does that piece of chocolate cake tempt you? James (1:13–18) suggests the problem isn't in the cake. It's in the fact that we love chocolate. It is the same way with temptations to do wrong. It isn't what's out there that's to blame. It is the fact that we are attracted to it. James added another thought. That temptation is actually a good gift given us by God. By resisting the temptation and doing what is right, we not only honor him, but we also become stronger and better persons.

1 Peter—Suffering Saints

By AD 64, life had changed for Christians. For decades, Christianity was viewed as a branch of Judaism. As Judaism was a legally recognized religion, Christians had been safe from persecution. But by 64, Christians were viewed as a different breed, followers of a religion that had no legal standing. Provincial governors had initiated pockets of persecution. In other places, there was a general hostility due in part to Christians' unpatriotic refusal to worship the empire's deities. Peter, near the end of his life, realized that more suffering lay ahead. He wrote this letter to provide perspective and to give encouragement to the persecuted.

Suffering

Over the centuries, Christians have been troubled by the problem of pain and suffering. Why, when all that believers desire is to lead peaceful lives and remain free to worship God, has there been so much persecution? Why, in many parts of the modern world, are so many Christians still suffering for their faith?

Even more troubling, perhaps, is the question of why individuals who try to do the right thing often find that everything seems to go wrong. Why does chronic illness rob a parent of the job he needs to support his family? Why does an accident take a loved one? There is seldom an answer to such questions. But 1 Peter provides perspective on our suffering and teaches us how to respond when suffering comes.

Always let others see you behaving properly, even though they may still accuse you of doing wrong. Then on the day of judgment, they will honor God by telling the good things they saw you do.

1 Peter 2:12 CEV

It is no shame to suffer for being a Christian. Praise God for the privilege of being called by his name!

1 Peter 4:16 NLT

Remember Who You Are (1 Peter 1:3–2:12)

The book of 1 Peter opens with a reminder of who we are in Jesus. We are those who have been born again and promised an inheritance in heaven. We have been saved; God is at work in us; and we experience his joy. As God's children, we are called to be holy. We are to break out of the mold that shapes the majority and be holy in all that we do. We are to live, not for the things of this world, but in expectation of Jesus' return. We are a chosen people, a royal priesthood, called to praise the one who chose us.

Walk the Way of Submission (1 Peter 2:13–3:7)

As the people of God, we are free to obey God. And God has decreed that in this world his people are to be subject to human authorities. Whether a ruler is just or unjust, the Christian is to "put up with it for God's sake when you're treated badly for no good reason" (1 Peter 2:19 MSG).

This instruction of Peter's is rooted in the conviction that God is in control of whatever happens to us. God has placed us in our situation that we might follow the example of Jesus, who also suffered for doing good. Like Jesus, we are to entrust ourselves to God.

Suffering for Doing Good (1 Peter 3:8–4:2)

Peter didn't want us to assume that Christians always suffer. In fact, because God supervises the outcome of our actions, normally, doing the right thing will have positive results. Yet, at times, doing good will lead to suffering. How should we handle such experiences?

First, Peter advised us to look on suffering as a blessing. He said not to be afraid, to remember that Jesus is Lord. Jesus is in charge, and what is happening is his will. Therefore, remain upbeat and positive, something observers will never understand, and that will provide opportunities to share our hope in Jesus.

Peter concluded by pointing to Jesus. He was innocent, and yet he, rather than the guilty men who accused him, suffered on the cross. God used this injustice to bring us to God. Surely the one who transformed the injustice of the Cross into a blessing intends to bless us through the things we suffer.

Look Beyond Today (1 Peter 4:3–11)

The end of all things is near. Those who persecute us will be judged. Until then we are to focus on loving and serving one another.

Suffering as Christians (1 Peter 4:12–19)

There is no benefit in bearing up under suffering that is deserved. But bearing up under unjust suffering is participation in Jesus' sufferings. So, Peter admonished, don't be surprised when suffering comes, as if it were something strange. Commit yourself to God, and keep on doing what is good.

> Casting all your anxiety on Him, because He cares for you.
>
> 1 Peter 5:7 NASB

Concluding Remarks (1 Peter 5:1–14)

Peter concluded with words of exhortation, reminding his readers that after they have suffered "a little while" (1 Peter 5:10 NASB), God himself will restore them and make them strong.

Digging Deeper

The Greeks viewed suffering as an unmixed evil, thrust on a helpless humanity by an impersonal fate. Most Greek tragedies are rooted in this view, with the hero an unfortunate victim. The Bible has a different perspective. This is a moral universe. What happens to us is generally determined by our choices. But when undeserved suffering comes, God is at work to accomplish some good purpose in or through the experience. At the very least, such suffering allows us to participate in the suffering of Jesus. At best, our suffering will be transformed into blessing for us or for others.

Myth Buster

Every mention of *baptism* in the Bible isn't a reference to water. Baptism in 1 Peter 3:21–4:2 refers to union with Jesus (Romans 6:1-7; 1 Corinthians 12:13), not water baptism. Peter drew an analogy with the Genesis Flood. Just as the ark carried Noah through the waters of judgment and deposited him in a new world, so union with Jesus carries us safely past God's judgment and deposits us in a new spiritual universe, where we live in accordance with the will of God. The reference to the "spirits now in prison" (1 Peter 3:19 NASB) is to the men and women of Noah's time, to whom Jesus spoke through the ark-builder.

Final Thoughts

Peter says, "Do not fear what they fear" (1 Peter 3:14 NIV). Most of the world fears suffering as an unavoidable evil. But God sometimes uses suffering to strengthen us and make us more sensitive to others. Christians can take comfort in the knowledge that God is near and that he is in charge.

2 Peter—Against Heresy

Peter probably wrote this letter shortly before his execution in Rome in AD 68. To Peter, the presence of false teachers in the church seemed to pose a greater threat than the persecution by pagans that he dealt with in his first letter. Second Peter strongly resembles 2 Timothy and the epistle of Jude. All three, written after Christianity had spread throughout Roman lands, warn against the danger of false teachers and encourage their recipients to stand firm in the faith.

God's Part and Ours (2 Peter 1)

God has given us everything we need for life and godliness, infusing us with his own life and giving us his reliable Word. Our part is to "make every effort" (2 Peter 1:5 NIV) to nurture qualities that make us effective, productive believers. Specifically, on the foundation of faith, we are to add goodness, knowledge, self-control, perseverance, godliness, brotherly kindness, and love (1:5-7).

Everything that goes into a life of pleasing God has been miraculously given to us by getting to know, personally and intimately, the One who invited us to God.

2 Peter 1:3 MSG

The Lord knows how to rescue the godly from trials and to keep the unrighteous under punishment until the day of judgment,

2 Peter 2:9 HCSB

False Teachers (2 Peter 2)

The Christian community had been infiltrated by false teachers who were spreading heresies. False teachers could be recognized by their doctrine, their lifestyle, and their teaching. They denied the lordship of Jesus and his sacrifice. And they were motivated by greed, exploiting those who followed them. They were arrogant and followed "the corrupt desires of the sinful nature and despise[d] authority" (2:10 NIV). They promised the followers "freedom" (2:19 NIV) and appealed to "the lustful desires of sinful human nature" (2:18 NIV).

The End of the World (2 Peter 3)

The corrective to false teaching is to remember that the world is about to end in a cataclysmic divine judgment. The universe itself will "disappear with a roar" (2 Peter 3:10 NIV) in a gigantic fireball, and God will create a new heaven and a new earth to be the home of righteousness. In view of this, Christians should be motivated to live godly and holy lives.

Final Thoughts

A focus on Jesus' return and the end of this world provides a practical benefit. It can help to make us immune to the promises of false teachers, who emphasize the supposed benefits they can help us gain in this world—benefits that seem attractive but have no truly lasting benefit.

Dictionary

heresy *(n.)* 1. The denial of central doctrines of Scripture. 2. The promotion of a sinful lifestyle.

1 John—Experiencing Daily Fellowship with God

The apostle John was an old man, the last survivor of the twelve apostles, when he wrote these epistles. In this letter and two brief notes, John focused on a unique aspect of Christianity. The believer has the potential of experiencing daily fellowship with God. As John began his letter, he stated his purpose. John wrote "so that you may have fellowship with us. And our fellowship is with the Father and with his Son, Jesus Christ" (1 John 1:3 NLT).

A Promise Remembered

The evening before the Crucifixion, Jesus shared a last supper with his disciples. At that time he told them, "If anyone loves Me, he will keep My word; and My Father will love him, and We will come to him and make Our abode with him" (John 14:23 NASB). In all the long decades that followed, John lived in the presence of God. In this letter he intended to share the secret.

> If anyone does sin, we have an advocate with the Father—Jesus Christ the righteous One.
>
> 1 John 2:1 HCSB
>
> Stay with what you heard from the beginning, the original message. Let it sink into your life.
>
> 1 John 2:24 MSG

John's letter isn't carefully reasoned like Paul's. John touches on topics and keeps coming back to them. Yet the main themes are clear. To experience the presence of Jesus, we need to live in light, live in love, and live by faith.

Live in Light (1 John 1:5–2:29)

Confessing sins (1:5–2:2). In this letter, as in John's Gospel, light stands in contrast with darkness. And God is light. He illumines all and sees everything clearly. To live in the light means to view things as God views them. Darkness represents a distorted view of reality. John called us to apply this concept and to face the truth about ourselves. No one who lives in darkness has fellowship with Jesus, and a person who claims to be sinless is definitely in darkness. John's advice? Stop deceiving yourself and trying to deceive others. Confess your sins to God, knowing that Jesus is faithful and will forgive your sins and continue cleansing you of unrighteousness.

Love others, not the world (2:3–29). Jesus commanded us to love one another (compare John 13:34–35). If you hate (reject) your brother, you're in darkness. If your passion is directed toward the cravings that motivate sinful man, if you're intent on gaining the things you can see and touch, if you're proud of mere possessions, you love the world, not your brothers and sisters.

Living in light is all about being honest concerning our sins and valuing others rather than things.

Live in Love (1 John 3:1–4:21)

God has shared his nature with those who believe in Jesus. And by nature God is love. God's love is more than affection. It is a passionate concern for others that drives us to seek what's best for them, even  as love drove Jesus to the Cross for our sake. In this section of his letter, John again emphasized the same themes. Trust Jesus, love one another, and obey his commands (1 John 3:23). John wrote, "Whoever lives in love lives in God" (4:16 NIV). Love is the way to stay close to Jesus. As we love, our confidence in God grows and we see answers to prayer. John ended this section with a reminder: "Whoever loves God must also love his brother" (4:21 NIV).

Live in Faith (1 John 5)

Believing in Jesus as the Christ provides a new birth, and we become God's children (1 John 5:1). God stated that if we have faith in his Son, he has given us eternal life. That's life now, not just life in the future.

God wants us to know that we have been given eternal life and that he hears our prayers.

The life that God gives us is dynamic. The fact is that infused with God's life we will not make a habit of sinning. "Because of Jesus, we now belong to the true God who gives eternal life" (1 John 5:20 CEV).

Life and the Experience of God's Presence

Trust in what God has said about his Son provides life and brings us into God's family. Many Christians fail to live with a sense of God's presence, and yet this experience is open to every believer. John's prescription was simple. Obey God, but be honest with yourself and with him when you sin. Confess your sins, and he'll forgive and continue to transform you. Take special care to nurture your love for fellow believers. Concentrate on loving others as Jesus loved you, and you will begin to sense Jesus' presence in your life.

> I write these things to you who believe in the name of the Son of God so that you may know that you have eternal life.
>
> 1 John 5:13 NIV

Something to Ponder

Two brief notes—2 and 3 John—follow John's first letter. In each, the key word is *truth*. In both epistles, the underlying concept is that to be true, something must ultimately be in harmony with reality. In this sense, truth is a partner to light, which is so prominent in John's first letter. Walking in the truth and living in light are essentially the same thing. John, who loves his fellow believers deeply, said that he had no greater joy than receiving reports that they were walking in the truth.

Digging Deeper

Like Peter and Jude, John is concerned about false teachers that infiltrate Christian communities, and so he provides a simple theological test. If a person denies that Jesus has come in the flesh—that is, if he says that Jesus is not God and human—that person is a false teacher (1 John 4:2-3). Though simple, the test is decisive. It is a test that can be applied today, and it will identify the majority of those who distort and corrupt the Christian faith.

Myth Buster

It's common for some to claim that the Gospels were written long after the supposed writers had died and that they present a Jesus idealized by later generations. This can't be claimed of John's writings. The apostle John lived late into the AD 90s, and a manuscript of part of John's Gospel, labeled P-38, dates from that decade. When we compare the teachings of John's Gospel and that of much later letters, we see the same themes and the same portrait of Jesus in each. John insisted that the first test to apply to those who claim to convey religious truth is whether or not they acknowledge "that Jesus Christ has come in the flesh" (1 John 4:2 NIV), God come to live among us. This is the consistent testimony of each Gospel writer and of the first-century church.

Final Thoughts

John began his letter by holding out the promise of an experience of Jesus' presence in our daily lives. The confidence that God is with us and that we can feel him near is a great gift. John reminds us that we receive this gift as we live in light, in love, and in faith.

Jude—Contending for the Faith

Jude was an old man when he wrote this brief letter to fellow believers. He had planned to write about the salvation they enjoy, but as he began, his thoughts drifted to the false teachers who were troubling Christian communities in the 80s. His pen flew over the papyrus pages, and the words poured out; powerful words of condemnation, and then a calmer call to his readers to contend for their faith.

✳

Condemnation of False Teachers (Jude 1–16)

Some two decades earlier, Paul and Peter had predicted the proliferation of divisive teachers (2 Timothy; 2 Peter). By the mid 80s, they seemed to be everywhere, divisive influences who "change the grace of our God into a license for immorality and deny Jesus Christ our only Sovereign and Lord" (Jude 4 NIV). Both apostles had described the characteristics of false teachers in this same way, focusing on their loose lifestyles and denial of Jesus' deity.

The false teachers were destined for judgment and eternal fire (Jude 5-7). Like unreasoning animals, they had no awareness of spiritual realities (8-10). They walked in the footsteps of sacred history's greatest villains (11). And, in a series of graphic images, Jude pointed out that for all their claims, they produced nothing of value (12-16).

A servant of the Lord must not quarrel but must be kind to everyone, be able to teach, and be patient with difficult people. Gently instruct those who oppose the truth. Perhaps God will change those people's hearts, and they will learn the truth.

2 Timothy 2:24–25 NLT

You, dear friends, must build each other up in your most holy faith.

Jude 20 NLT

Contending for the Faith (Jude 17–23)

Normally we think of contending as confronting, arguing, or even physically battling. Jude recognized a better way. Believers were to concentrate on building themselves up in their faith, to pray in the Holy Spirit, to keep themselves in God's love, to expect Jesus' return, to be merciful to those who had doubts, and to seek to save others.

Doxology (Jude 24–25)

Jude closed with praise of the one who is able to keep authentic believers from falling and bring them safely to heaven.

Final Thoughts

We can sense Jude's outrage at the false teachers of his day. It's natural to be wary when we are convinced that someone is distorting important truths. But Jude wisely concluded that the Christian's best protection against false teachers is to focus on understanding and living his or her own Christian faith.

Digging Deeper

The book of Enoch was a well-known religious writing that neither Jew nor Christian viewed as Scripture, but it did affect the way Jews viewed many Old Testament events. Jude referred to this book (Jude 14). He was not quoting such writings as authoritative; rather, he wanted to point out that the false teachers misunderstood even these stories. Correctly understood, even those religious writings supported a traditional understanding of the Old Testament.

Revelation—The Final Triumph

In the last decade of the first century during the reign of the emperor Domitian, the apostle John was exiled to the Island of Patmos. He was in his nineties. As John prayed one Sunday, he was given an unexpected vision. In John's own words, his vision was "a revelation [an unveiling] of Jesus Christ," whose intent was "to show his servants what must soon take place" (Revelation 1:1 NIV). There is no more-controversial book in the New Testament, nor one that is more full of vivid and difficult-to-understand images.

✳

Three Distinct Sections

The events in Revelation are presented as threefold: what has been, what is now, and what will be.

Revelation 1. John fell on his knees before the awesome figure of Jesus in his full resurrection glory. John was told to write down what he had seen, what was now, and what would "take place" (1:19 NKJV).

Revelation 2-3. Jesus dictated letters to seven churches. Each described the present state of a congregation. Many commentators view these churches as representative of eras in church history.

To Him who loved us and washed us from our sins in His own blood, and has made us kings and priest to His God and Father, to Him be glory and dominion forever and ever.

Revelation 1:5–6 NKJV

I saw the dead, both great and small, standing before God's throne. . . . And the dead were judged according to what they had done, as recorded in the books.

Revelation 20:12 NLT

Revelation 4-22. This third and longest section of Revelation is the focus of interpretative debate. While some view chapters 4–22 as a description of what will take place hereafter, others differ.

Four Views of Revelation 4–22

Across the centuries, four different views of this major section of Revelation have been proposed:

1. *Preterist view: Revelation is a veiled attack on the Roman Empire.* This view discounts any predictive element in Revelation. "Babylon" and the "beasts" represent Rome and lie under divine judgment.

2. *Historicist view: Revelation is a preview of church history.* One branch of this view identifies elements of John's vision with historical events between the first and eighteenth centuries. The other branch divides chapters 4–22 into seven visions, each of which recapitulates God's ultimate triumph.

3. *Futurist view: Revelation is a prophetic look into the future.* This view sees the phrase "what will take place after this" (1:19 NKJV) as the key. These nineteen chapters describe future events.

4. *Idealist view: Revelation is a purely symbolic representation of the struggle between good and evil.* This view sees all persons and events described as symbolic expressions of the conviction that good will triumph over evil.

It is clear from the radically differing views that the understanding of Revelation varies greatly.

Problems for Interpreters

There are two problems for all the interpretative schools. First, John used abundant symbols. While many of the symbols were drawn from the Old Testament and others were explained in Revelation itself, we're still forced to guess at what many symbols represent. Second, John must rely on simile. This is even more serious.

Picture a New England farmer of 1700 who has been given a vision of Chicago's O'Hare International Airport of 2010. He tries to share his vision. But the farmer has no names for what he has seen, and there is nothing truly comparable in his own time. The best he can do is to say something like, "I saw a tube with wings. Smoke and fire came out of the wings and lifted the tube into the air."

> The one who has spoken these things says, "I am coming soon!"
>
> Revelation 22:20 CEV

That was John's problem. He described what he saw. But the best he could do was report that "the sky receded like a scroll, rolling up" (Revelation 6:14 NIV). John saw *something*. It certainly wasn't a scroll, rolling up. But he was forced to say it was "like" something his contemporaries were familiar with. Thus, we should not expect to understand John's images until the things he described come to pass.

How Should We Read Revelation 4–22?

First, it is not necessary to understand everything we read in any Bible book. We will always have unanswered questions, and so we shouldn't be put off by what we don't understand. Second, much in Revelation is clear enough, such as the many images of judgment or John's vision of heaven and hell. Read Revelation for what you can understand. Third, read chapters 4–22 at one sitting. You'll be overwhelmed by the conviction that God intends to judge humankind's sin and put an end to evil in his universe. Reading through these chapters several times creates a healthy sense of awe and helps us set priorities in our own lives. Finally, if you want answers to your questions about Revelation, buy several commentaries and compare the viewpoints.

Digging Deeper

Revelation is the only book of the Bible that warns readers to add nothing to, and subtract nothing from, "this book of prophecy" (Revelation 22:18–19 NIV). It's also the only book of the Bible that announces a blessing on "everyone who pays attention to the message of this book" (Revelation 22:7 CEV). Clearly Revelation should have a special place in our Scripture reading.

Symbols in Revelation

Symbol	Text in Revelation	Represents
Seven burning lamps	4:5	Spirit of God
Bowls of incense	5:8	Prayers of the saints
Great dragon	12:9	Satan
Seven heads	17:9	Seven hills
Waters	17:15	People, nations

Old Testament Symbols in Revelation

Symbol	Text in Revelation	Text in Old Testament	Represents
Rod of iron	2:27	Psalm 2:9	Jesus' rule
Morning star	2:28	Daniel 12:3	Reign with Jesus
Key of David	3:7	Isaiah 22:22	Messiah's authority
Four horsemen	6:1	Zechariah 1:8; Ezekiel 5:17	God's purposes; Ezekiel carried out
Rainbow	10:1	Genesis 9:13	God's mercy

Biblical Meaning and Purpose

Neither pleasure, wealth, nor power can give meaning to a life lived in a meaningless universe, where death means extinction and every individual's destiny is to be forgotten.

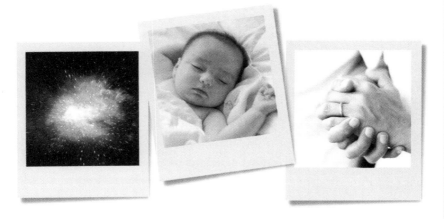

Contents

Intentional Creation 247

Significance in Human Life 249

God's View 251

I will meditate on Your precepts and think about Your ways.
I will delight in Your statutes; I will not forget Your word.

Psalm 119:15–16 HCSB

Intentional Creation

Is there meaning and purpose to human life? Let's assume that this universe is an accident, fashioned by an unexplainable event that took place fifteen to twenty billion years ago. Life emerged from the random mixing of lifeless elements that by mere chance became alive. That original bit of living matter pulled itself from primordial slime and began its journey upward, organizing itself into more and more complex patterns by processes no one can explain. In popularizing this theory, contemporary "science" has robbed moderns of meaning and purpose.

Implications

The view described above leads to an erosion of hope. If chance rules, we humans are helpless victims of meaningless events that lie beyond our control. Ecclesiastes records Solomon's struggles to find some meaning in a life lived without reference to a Creator. His search drove him to conclude that all is meaningless.

The Biblical View

The Bible presents a very different view of origins. The universe is the intentional creation of an all-powerful Person, God. God not only created the universe, he also populated it with living creatures. As the climax of creation, God made humans in his own image and likeness.

> This is what God the LORD says—who created the heavens and stretched them out, who spread out the earth and what comes from it, who gives breath to the people on it and life to those who walk on it—"I, the LORD, have called you."
>
> Isaiah 42:5–6 HCSB
>
> I declare the end from the beginning, and from long ago what is not yet done, saying: My plan will take place, and I will do all My will.
>
> Isaiah 46:10 HCSB

God's creation of the universe was not an end in itself. The universe is a stage on which the drama of sin and salvation are being played out. When the play is over and the curtain falls, this universe will be dismantled. The evils Satan and humans have introduced will be eradicated, and the billions who have trusted God will file out of the theater for an endless life of joy in the presence of the Creator.

This biblical view also has powerful implications. Seemingly random events are the Author's work, and his hidden hand shapes them for his purposes. Now the way we play our part matters, for our experience in eternity hinges on whether the choices we make are in harmony or in conflict with God's purposes. Truly, Christian believers and secular humans live in different worlds.

Final Thoughts

Christian interpretations of the Creation account in Genesis 1 differ. Some believe the seven days of creation represent consecutive twenty-four-hour periods; others believe that they represent periods of divine activity followed by ages of development. But we agree that God created, and this infuses all creation with a sense of purpose.

Check Your Understanding

- **Some view the universe and human life as the products of random chance. What are the implications of this view?**

If chance rules, there is no meaning or purpose in the universe. We are victims of random events we cannot control. The choices we make ultimately make no real difference.

- **The Bible views the universe and human life as intentionally caused by God for purposes he has revealed. What are the implications of this view?**

If God created the universe with a purpose, human life has significance. Our choices will be either in harmony or in conflict with his purposes, and will have a powerful impact on our experience.

Significance in Human Life

The world in which believers live is strange to many people. For us the present takes on significance because we realize how brief today is. Our destiny is eternity; our life on earth a journey toward the celebration of a grand reunion with God. We see our joys and even our tragedies as gifts of divine providence, threads in a grand tapestry whose final shape we see but dimly now, but whose beauty will one day be revealed. We do not choose the role we play in the realization of God's plan, but we know that we have a role. To play that role well and to God's glory gives our lives meaning and purpose.

✳

Finding Personal Meaning and Purpose

Millions of people have found meaning and purpose for their lives in their relationship with God. They realize that they are important to God for themselves and not just for what they can accomplish. The Bible speaks of human beings as God's treasured possessions (Exodus 19:5; Deuteronomy 7:6). There is no longer any question of struggling to deserve God's love. Believers have recognized the love of God in Jesus, and are convinced that God's love will never be withdrawn (Romans 8:38-39).

We also have as our ambition, whether at home or absent, to be pleasing to Him.

2 Corinthians 5:9 NASB

Throw yourselves into the work of the Master, confident that nothing you do for him is a waste of time or effort.

1 Corinthians 15:58 MSG

Awareness of God's love kindles our love for him, and this love motivates us to be followers of Jesus. We do not know how we fit into God's grand plan; we concentrate daily on making it our goal to please him. We look to him to meet our needs. We strive to love others as he loves us. We find material possessions less and less attractive. Rather than be consumed by a desire for things, we gain deeper and lasting satisfaction in service to others. The purpose that gives our lives meaning is the desire to please and glorify God.

Strangely, perhaps, we discover greater pleasure in the good things of this life—in family, friends, work, laughter, love—than do those who pursue pleasure as an end in itself.

Final Thoughts

 Luther said it. "Love God, and do as you please." Love provides the perspective on life that we all need. Love moves us to choose what pleases God and is of service to others. Ultimately, this is what gives our lives purpose and meaning.

Check Your Understanding

- **What perspective shapes the Christian's priorities.**

The Christian's priorities are shaped by the perspective that our destiny is in eternity and orders our preferences in this life in view of eternity.

- **How does love transform the Christian's experience, and what is the outcome of a life lived to love God and serve others?**

Being assured of God's love for us, we no longer struggle to earn our salvation. Instead, moved by God's love, we are motivated to please God and to serve others. Our lives are given meaning and purpose, and we find pleasure in the good things of this life.

God's View

One of the questions that the Bible raises is this: What gives the universe meaning and purpose to God? Another way of asking this is: What goals of God are being accomplished in creating and sustaining this universe? Too often we approach such questions from a human-centered point of view. In fact, the God whom Scripture reveals is the central figure in history's unfolding drama. Humans are not. We can't begin to answer questions about God's purposes unless we understand that it's appropriate and right for God to act for his own glory, honor, and praise.

✳

Glory, Praise, and Honor

God is a God of revelation. Scripture says that from the beginning he has made known his power and deity through the things he made. And the appropriate response, glorifying and thanking God, has been denied him by fallen human beings who "suppress" this truth (compare Romans 1:18–20).

In fact, we can see all of sacred history as a progressive revelation by God of himself, in search of the praise, glory, and honor that are his due. As event follows event, we see fresh facets of God's character and personality. In Eden, we see God's mercy shown the fallen pair. In God's promise to Abraham, kept through the ages, we see God's faithfulness. In the Genesis Flood,

This is eternal life: that they may know you, the only true God, and Jesus Christ, whom you have sent.

John 17:3 NIV

Praise, honor, glory, and strength forever and ever to the one who sits on the throne and to the Lamb!

Revelation 5:13 CEV

we see his commitment to justice. In Jesus' death on the cross, we see the triumph of love. Ultimately, when Jesus returns, we will see sin and evil purged and put away, and we will see death itself surrender to a resurrection life that is God's own. In every recorded act, God is displayed to us.

This view even helps us understand the problem of evil. Why does God permit it? Why not simply unleash his power and do away with it? Perhaps because it is only against the backdrop of evil that we can understand what it means for God to be Good. And perhaps only in concert with suffering can God display his compassion.

Final Thoughts

As we read the Bible, let us be alert for every glimpse of God. We will never fully understand him. But as we learn more about who he is and what his purposes are, we will be moved to give him the glory, praise, and honor that are his due.

Check Your Understanding

- **What makes it hard for us to grasp God's purposes in the universe, especially when we have the problem of evil?**

We tend to look at things from a human-centered point of view, which makes it difficult to understand God's purposes. As the true nature of evil expresses itself in our world, however, we can better understand God as good in the contrast.

- **What is the appropriate motive for God's actions, and how does God bring himself glory, praise, and honor?**

It is appropriate that God acts in order to bring himself glory, praise, and honor. He does this by revealing aspects of his character in his actions.

God, after He spoke long ago to the fathers in the prophets in many portions and in many ways, in these last days has spoken to us in His Son, whom He appointed heir of all things, through whom also He made the world.

Hebrews 1:1–2 NASB

Nobody ever outgrows Scripture; the book widens
and deepens with our years.

Charles H. Spurgeon

As the Scriptures say . . . "The word of the Lord remains forever."
And that word is the Good News.

1 Peter 1:24–25 NLT

God means what he says. What he says goes. His powerful Word is sharp as a surgeon's scalpel, cutting through everything, whether doubt or defense, laying us open to listen and obey. Nothing and no one is impervious to God's Word. We can't get away from it—no matter what.

Hebrews 4:12–13 MSG

Books in
The Indispensable Guide to Practically Everything
series include:

The Indispensable Guide to Practically Everything: The Bible

The Indispensable Guide to Practically Everything: World Religions and What People Believe